Down Your Street
Cambridge Past and Present

Volume II
East Cambridge

Sara Payne

THE PEVENSEY PRESS
Cambridge England

Published by The Pevensey Press
6 De Freville Avenue, Cambridge CB4 1HR, UK

© The Pevensey Press, 1984

ISBN 0 907115 19 5

The major parts of the chapters in this book and most of the
accompanying photographs previously appeared in the *Cambridge
Weekly News*, and the author and publishers wish to thank
Cambridge Newspapers Ltd for their co-operation. The generous
provision of information and illustrations by the Cambridgeshire
Collection, Cambridgeshire Libraries, is gratefully acknowledged.

The author and publishers also wish to thank the following for
the loan of photographs: City of Cambridge Department of
Architecture and Planning (p. 16, p. 41); Mrs Kathleen Apthorpe
Webb (p. 22); M. Betterman (p. 48); Cambridge and County Folk
Museum (p. 51); Robin Cox (p. 110); Donald MacKay (p. 112);
Albert Scott (p. 114, p. 115).

Map on pp. 72–73 by Jon Harris

Edited by Ruth Smith
Designed by Jim Reader
Design and production in association
with Book Production Consultants, Cambridge

Typesetting in Times Roman by Westholme Graphics Ltd
Printed in Great Britain at the University Press, Cambridge

Front cover: Fitzroy Street in about 1903 and (above) in 1984

Frontispiece: Part of Baker's map of Cambridge in 1830, from the
hand-coloured original in the Cambridgeshire Collection: note the
absence of houses

Down Your Street

Contents

Foreword

To many people outside and some inside, Cambridge is synonymous with its historic centre, that unique amalgam of splendid and seemingly calm College and University buildings encircling a higgledy-piggledy but intensely active shopping and commercial core. In her first collection of articles, Sara Payne wrote about this area. Not that it has not been written about before. Everything from weighty tomes of architectural description and historical analysis at one end of the spectrum to detective stories set among gabled cloisters at the other has been poured out ceaselessly. Perhaps, however, because the last forty years have seen fundamental changes in both the fabric of the centre and the ways of life of its people there has recently been a growing interest in recording what might be called social history – that mixture of anecdote and personal reminiscence which Sara carries off with insight, journalistic skill and wit.

This second collection of articles deals with another Cambridge – parts that the tourists and visitors rarely see unless they have misread the map. It is essentially about town rather than gown Cambridge, and encompasses the Kite Area, St Matthew's and Romsey lying to the east of the centre and out as far as Coldham's Common. Unlike the centre, its urban history is short. Until the early-19th-century Enclosure Act released sites for building, the area was predominantly in agricultural use, a relic of the great field system which had surrounded the medieval town. The Cambridgeshire Collection has a splendid series of maps from which one can chart the spread of development. Baker's map of 1830 shows a cluster of small streets and houses on either side of East Road. Mill Road had a mill, but precious little else. By 1863 the railway had arrived but there did not appear to be an instant surge of development in that direction. That does not show until the famous Cambridge Chronicle Map of 1899. By then the majority of the streets and houses in St Matthew's had been built, there was frontage development along most of Mill Road, and the heartland of Romsey town, as it had become

known by the mid 1880s, was all there. There were substantial areas in the north of St Matthew's and Romsey which were still open and the word "allotments" appears often, no doubt partly as a result of the large population of railwaymen in the area. The remainder of the open land was not developed until after the war.

My personal connections with the area are sparse – I had a great-uncle who lived in Ainsworth Street and my two children were born in the Mill Road Maternity Hospital – but professionally I have been involved with it in varying degrees over the last 16 years. For the whole of that time I have been embroiled in the saga of the shopping development in the Kite Area. I think it is fair to say that the Kite Area suffered from Cambridge's equivalent of the Thirty Years' War and certainly belied its name on Baker's map, the Garden of Eden. The future of the area is now more settled, the residential parts have an assured future, the great majority of the houses have been improved and the Grafton Centre is a successful implant which has brought new architecture, new life and new employment to the heart of the area.

St Matthew's and Romsey have also been intensively studied – although mercifully not over such a protracted time-scale – and I believe that there is a large measure of agreement over the improvements that both areas need and a steady programme for doing what can be done.

Against this background, I find Sara Payne's series totally absorbing; it's a bit like opening a previously locked cupboard in a familiar room and finding it full of extra information about who had used the room and why. At the end of a fascinating read, you have learnt a lot, met many new people, seen the past come to life in pictures and words, and most of all enjoyed yourself. May Sara have many more cupboards to open, please.

D. W. Urwin, M.A., M.R.T.P.I.
Chief Planning Officer
Cambridge City Council   June 1984

Preface

This book is about the Kite, that area of urban, residential Cambridge whose future was the subject of so much dissention and debate in the 1960s and 1970s. While the article on Fitzroy Street was being researched and written the bulldozers were moving in to flatten homes and small businesses there and in neighbouring James Street, ready for the creation of the Grafton Centre, Cambridge's second shopping centre – which was officially opened on 20 October 1983, the day *Down Your Street* vol. I, *Central Cambridge*, was published.

The bulldozers razed buildings, but they did not destroy a sense of corporate identity. It is memories of the Kite, from Victorian times to the days of the second world war, that I have tapped to plot the history of this locality, which used to depend entirely on hard-working artisans for its livelihood.

A strong community spirit also characterises the densely populated streets in the adjacent areas of Barnwell, St Matthew's and Romsey Town. Their numerous, exceedingly modest terrace houses were home to generations of craftsmen, shopkeepers and railway workers, who were attracted to the town after the railway first came to Cambridge, and who raised their large families here. The University vetoed several central localities that were suggested for the station. A spot to the south-east of the City finally proved acceptable, and the railway township of Romsey grew up around it. Many of the houses were built for the grandparents of a surviving generation of railway men who can trace the history of these streets with authentic, enlivening detail.

As with volume I, I am once again enormously indebted to a great many individuals who have given me immeasurable help with details about this key residential area of Cambridge. Without their collaboration, much valuable social history would have been lost forever. The published sources I have referred to (other than basic reference works such as street directories) are listed in the Bibliography at the end of the book.

Of my helpers, I would once again like to thank Cambridge Newspapers Ltd and my colleagues there for all their continued co-operation. The unflagging support from the editorial staff of the *Cambridge Weekly News*, in particular the editor, Gordon Richards, and the sub-editor Colin Moule, is constantly encouraging and gratifying. To all the photographic staff, especially Paul Craske, and to the librarian Denis Long, thank you for all your help.

Again the Cambridgeshire Collection of the Cambridge Central Library and the County Record Office have been essential sources of information. And again I would say that both the series and this book would have been impossible without the tireless assistance of Michael Petty, the librarian of the Cambridgeshire Collection, and his staff. I am grateful to them and to Michael Farrar, the county archivist, and his deputies, and to Richard Wilson, curator of the Folk Museum.

I would like to thank also the many local residents, past and present, who have helped me to compile these articles, in particular Leonard Amey and Bert Forsdyke of Romsey Town. I am most grateful to the *News* readers who have added copious additional memories and details. Points from their letters have, where possible, been incorporated into the chapters in this volume.

The Pevensey Press continues to have faith in the series by making it available in book form. Once again, Ruth Smith has edited the text in a masterly fashion.

This book is dedicated to my husband David, and our children Rose and Julian.

Sara Payne
Cambridge, 1984

1 Abbey Road

14 May 1981

A historical pageant of epic proportions, ranging from Crusader knights and Augustinian monks to a Tudor physician and 18th-century landowners, marks the passage of history in the Abbey Road area of Barnwell, one of the most historic parts of Cambridge. The pageant unfolds when you visit City Council tenant Professor Peter Danckwerts in Abbey Road's stately home, Abbey House. Yards from the race-track roundabout and the fumes of Elizabeth Way, once rural Walnut Tree Avenue, down which the dairymen drove their cows towards the Common, is this beautiful rambling house full of enough historical associations to fill many books, which of course have been written.

Professor Danckwerts, who is former Shell Professor of Chemical Engineering, is about to publish "The Inheritors of Barnwell Priory" for the Antiquarian Society, and you can buy a copy from him if you are interested. Many people would compete for my title of best historical raconteur; the award could go posthumously to Arthur Gray for his *Cambridge Revisited*, full of anecdotes wittily told. Professor Danckwerts, who has immersed himself in the history of Barnwell and the evolution of the area, would be another strong contender. It is the little details in his story that make it all so absorbing. The historical ambience of Abbey House, with its Tudor origins, is such that it is not difficult to visualise Barnwell Priory, founded in 1112, whose grounds appear, to quote Arthur Gray, "to have embraced the area extending from the site of Walnut Tree Avenue [now Elizabeth Way] to that of River Lane, bounded . . . on the north by the river and on the south by the main road".

Professor Danckwerts carries on the story. "The monks who built the Priory built the Abbey Church for the public to say Mass. Barnwell Abbey itself was the church of Barnwell Priory. This Abbey, 450 ft long, was not much smaller than King's College Chapel, which is 500 ft. The Abbey would have had cloisters and a fishpond." Professor Danckwerts told me how there had in fact been a small monastery on the site of Magdalene College from 1092, but the monks needed more space. Local landowner Pain Peverel (hence Peverel Road), a famous

soldier who had been standard-bearer to Robert, Duke of Normandy, during the First Crusade, acquired the 13 acres of land in Barnwell from Henry I and built the Priory of St Giles and St Andrew. Jumping forward a few centuries we come to rapacious Henry VIII and the dissolution of the monasteries in 1538. As Arthur Gray puts it, "Upon the dissolution of the Priory the building served as a convenient quarry. In 1578, when the Chapel of Corpus Christi College was being built, it is recorded that 182 loads of stone were removed from the dismantled monastery to the college." From 1553 until 1655 the Priory land was owned by the Wendys of Haslingfield, the local lords of the manor. Dr Thomas Wendy of Haslingfield was physician to four successive monarchs, including Henry VIII, whose will he witnessed. He bought a pardon from Mary Tudor for having treated Princess Elizabeth.

Abbey House apparently has no connection with the Priory, although there may be some of the stones in it. Professor Danckwerts said that it was probably first built in 1580, and that an extension dated externally 1678 was added by Ambrose Butler. The Butler family owned the Priory land and Abbey House from 1656 to 1759. The most notorious of these Butlers was Jacob, who inherited the property in 1714. He was called Squire Butler, was 6 ft 4 in tall and lived to the age of 85. At the time of his death he was the oldest barrister in England. In the huge hall of Abbey House, which is just being redecorated, Professor Danckwerts told me that it was here that Squire Butler used to keep his huge coffin (it was a double one), and he and his friends used to sit in it and drink wine, and wait for the "call".

The house has a wealth of fine 17th-century oak panelling. This would have replaced the Tudor plaster-work. The imported panelling in one of the bedrooms was said to have come from Jesus College, but Professor Danckwerts rather doubts that story. He thinks it is more likely to have come from Fen Ditton Hall, the home of the Panton

Abbey House: it dates from around 1580

anxious to enclose the open fields of Barnwell and then develop them. Leonard Amey, in his article on the Barnwell Fields, describes them as filling "practically the whole area between the built up town, the riverside grazings on two flanks, and the parish boundaries of Cherry Hinton and Trumpington". But Panton was opposed by the University, whose members, as Florence Ada Keynes says in her *By-Ways of Cambridge History*, "thought their rides would be curtailed, and consequently their health injured, if they could no longer gallop over the open fields adjoining Cambridge. In 1806 the bill for authorising the enclosure was carried through the House of Commons in spite of the opposition from the University." Mrs Keynes (mother of Maynard) explains the next stage of Abbey House history. "As 'Tommy' Panton left no heirs, his lands, including the Barnwell Priory estate, went to his niece, Lady Gwydir, daughter of the Duchess of Ancaster. In 1820 the whole property passed to Lady Gwydir's son, who sold it in lots to various persons – Fen Ditton, including Barnwell, was bought by Dr Haviland, a Cambridge doctor. The Barnwell property subsequently changed hands several times. The Abbey House found tenants, but the main part of the site remained practically unused and uncultivated."

Joseph Sturton, the philanthropic developer who gave his name to Sturton Street, bought the estate in 1879 and made roads and sold most of the land in small building plots. Enough was enclosed to form a garden for Abbey House. The only remnant of the Priory buildings, standing on a small plot of ground near the garden, was given by Mr Sturton to the Cambridge Antiquarian Society. It is known as the Cellarer's Checker (Exchequer, i.e. office). For many years Abbey House was divided into three parts, but in 1945 it was bought from the then owner, a Mr Askham, by Lord Fairhaven of Anglesey Abbey, who presented it to the Cambridge and County Folk Museum as "an expression of thanksgiving for the preservation of the nation" in the last war. The Folk Museum was unable to cope financially with its inheritance, so it gave the Abbey House to the City Council. The Danckwerts, who moved in as tenants in 1965, have negotiated (in the absence of a sale) a long lease with the Council, who cannot have vacant possession of the house until the year 2027. The Danckwerts are responsible for the interior, the Council for the exterior. Both have to defer to the National Trust, which is given jurisdiction over the upkeep and appearance by a clause in the title deeds. As Professor Danckwerts put it, "It is a great mistake to own a listed building – it is not a poor man's hobby!"

Miss Kathleen Morgan outside her home, 42 Abbey Road. Behind her can be seen the bricked-up doorway to her grandfather's boot and shoe workshop, which was at first-floor level

family, who bought Abbey House from the Butlers. Thomas Panton was chief groom or equerry to George II, and master of the King's running horses, which means that he was the King's trainer. His son "Polite" Tommy Panton was a steward of the Jockey Club and won the Derby in 1786. Apparently "Polite" Tommy – he was very suave – never missed an important race meeting.

As a big landowner Thomas Panton Jnr was

Back now to Joseph Sturton and the development in 1886 of Abbey Road. The object was to sell the plots with their 18 ft frontages for artisan dwellings, but according to Professor Danckwerts, "they didn't go with a swing". The houses were mostly built by a well-known local builder called Clark. Miss Kathleen Morgan has an interesting story to tell about her family home, 42 Abbey Road. "My grandfather built this house, it was one of the first to go up. Grandfather was a University shoemaker called Ellis John Rolls." (The street directory for 1891 describes Mr Rolls as a "boot closer".) Miss Morgan, a retired nurse, remembers being told that when the house was built there was a pit opposite. "They dug up fossils called coprolite which they used for manure." Grandfather Rolls built the house with his shoemaking business in mind. "The shoemaking room was on the first floor – we always called it the shop – and customers went up to the room via a ladder at the back of the house," said Miss Morgan. Her grandmother was obviously not going to have people traipsing up and down to the shop through the house, hence that ladder.

During the 1880s excavation of a Saxon barrow took place in nearby Priory and Saxon Roads. "The man who was supervising the dig used to come and sit in grandfather's shop and watch the progress." Among Mr Rolls' customers who came to be fitted at the bespoke shoemaker's were explorers and the cricketer Ranjee. Miss Morgan remembers as a child seeing the wooden lasts for the shoes hanging on the wall, and recalls the tub where her grandfather soaked some of the leathers for the shoes. "Mother told me that as a little girl she had a childish tantrum and grandfather sloshed her with a bit of wet leather from that tub." Miss Morgan's mother married a dairyman. "Father became a dairy farmer. They lived out at Fen Ditton Hall and then moved to Hardwick, but in the 1930s, because of hard times, we had to sell the farm and we came to live here." Miss Morgan went to school at Miss Royston's school on Newmarket Road.

The Rolls were very fond of the local children and were always entertaining them. Horace Lister, son of George Lister who set up the famous engineering works in Abbey Road in 1890, was one of the children who used to visit Grandfather Rolls. "Grandfather would give him pieces of leather for his spinning tops." Dodds' grocer's shop used to stand on the corner of Beche Road and Abbey Road. Subsequently it moved over to where the Cresta cleaners is now. Kathleen Morgan was friendly with the Dodds children. "Their uncle was the manager of the Victoria Cinema, so we used to get in there for nothing. Those were the days of

Mrs Evelyn Harris of Cresta Quality Cleaning

Charlie Chaplin, whose antics we would watch from the back row of the cinema. When we got home we would re-enact what we had seen on the screen in the back garden here under the apple trees." Miss Morgan remembers both sets of neighbours who lived in Abbey Road during her grandparents' time. "At no. 40 lived the man whom grandmother called 'Neighbour Mason', he was a shoemaker like grandfather. At no. 44 Mr Brown, who had a hansom cab business in Cambridge, kept his cab and horse." "Cuckoo" Dent was another local character. He was the ferryman who plied between the banks near the footbridge that leads into Manhattan Drive. Why "Cuckoo"? Miss Morgan knows that story. "They said that he used to go to bed for the whole winter and leave his son to do all the work. He only got up when he heard the first cuckoo!"

For years before it was built, there was a lot of talk about the site for the bridge which has since become known as the Elizabeth Way Bridge. At one time there were plans to run the approach road down Abbey Road, and build the bridge at that point over the river. You notice, if you go down and look, that the bank opposite the end of Abbey Road is free of building. The land was presumably bought up in anticipation of the bridge and then, once the decision came to site it a little further west, left undeveloped. Another Cambridge firm to have its offices in Abbey Road, like Listers, was Kidmans, the builders. The street directory for 1915 records that Charles Kidman lived at 1 Abbey Road, and Kidman and Sons, builders' contractors, had their offices at 3 Abbey Road.

Terrace houses, with their uniformity of style and architectural harmony, are often given an individual touch by their names. Abbey Road has its fair share of imposing-sounding residences. There is Gladstone House, built in 1887 (has anyone named their new home Thatcher House this year?), which belonged to the Lister family; they have since sold it to the Council. Vimiera House, next door at no. 38, is an interesting name, but I couldn't get to the bottom of that one, nor could Mrs Eley, who lives there. She is the widow of Mr Robert Eley, former secretary of the Conservative Club in Gwydir Street. The family who used to live at Harrogate House either came from Yorkshire or, perhaps, had a good holiday there. What about Valdora House? Roseville and Fern House are other names. It is fun to speculate on Victorian house names. There is enough history in Abbey Road to keep the antiquarians going.

2 Auckland Road

15 September 1983

Auckland Road, off Newmarket Road – dubbed "Hunstanton Beach" by the long-suffering residents who have had to wade through the sand and bricks of a mega house-building project taking place on the site of the old Maltings that once dominated the end of the road where it slopes down onto Midsummer Common – has adapted to many changes in the hundred years that have elapsed since it was first built on part of the Barnwell Fields of Cambridge.

Take first Auckland Road's theatre, where the early films of Charlie Chaplin were shown: the Hippodrome, which used to occupy the large warehouse that is now the workshops of Midsummer Glassmakers on the east side adjoining Midsummer Common. Simon Wood, the manager of Midsummer Glassmakers, which supplies such big London stores as Liberty's and Dickens and Jones with glassware, told me that "someone had come into our workshop and said that Charlie Chaplin had appeared at the Hippodrome here".

The Hippodrome in Auckland Road originally housed a circus called Tudor's Circus, which moved from Midsummer Common in about 1895. It was then renamed the Circus of Varieties, before becoming the Hippodrome where, according to Clifford Manning of Ely, an authority on cinemas in Cambridge, animated pictures were included as extra turns from 1896. The Hippodrome was owned by Thomas Askham, who aquired Tudor's Circus from William Tudor in 1900. Programmes presented at the Hippodrome from 1906 to 1909, says Mr Manning, included a visit by the Royal Italian Circus, who appeared in May 1906 and September 1907, and Poole's Myriorama, which came for a week in October 1907. Askham appears to have been a carriage builder and shoeing smith when he acquired Tudor's Circus. In 1910 he owned premises adjoining the Hippodrome described as a slaughterhouse and a builder's yard. He may also have been the owner of several boathouses, a quay, and the ferry at Chesterton, opposite Jesus Green.

What was the Hippodrome like? Probably a bit of a flea pit. Askham made several applications for a theatre licence, without success; in 1906, reporting the decision of the Theatre Committee against him, the *Cambridge Chronicle* for 22 June noted that there was no electric light at the Hippodrome, the nearest main being in James Street. The *Chronicle* of 27 July 1906 reported that Mr Askham wanted to cater for a lower class of working men and women than that catered for by the New Theatre in Newmarket Road. The licence he eventually got in 1908 still did not entitle him to stage plays; he was restricted to entertainments such as the circus.

The Hippodrome was rebuilt in 1913, and opened on Saturday 4 October as the Gaiety Theatre; this in turn closed two years later. In the 1920s the theatre

Auckland Road from Newmarket Road

was converted for commercial purposes. It was used as a garage by the Great Eastern Railway and Herbert Robinson, and later as a furniture warehouse by H.W. Peak and then Court Brothers Ltd. Cambridge Glassmakers acquired the lease of the warehouse in 1981, but ceased production in Christmas 1981. The leasehold and assets were then acquired by a new company, Midsummer Glassmakers, who are now successfully established there with the talented glassblower Dillon Clark heading the production team of four, who make everything from elegant clear glass drinking glasses, reminiscent of 17th- and 18th-century English crystal, to paperweights, bowls and glass animals. They accept special commissions too, and show parties round the workshop.

Auckland Road is perhaps best known for the brewery and malthouses (the posh new housing development there is called The Maltings) built about 100 years ago. The brewery was the Star Brewery, and the brewer Frederick Bailey. He lived and had his offices at 241 Newmarket Road, called Burleigh House. The Star Brewery had a large group of stables which were approached through the brewery yard in Auckland Road. The stables were built on either side of a paved courtyard, 90 ft long, roofed with glass. Alfred Barnard, in his account of the Star Brewery, says that the brewery stables were "model stables, as no expense had been spared either in their erection, ventilation, drainage, or fitting up. They contain accommodation for twenty horses, besides having mess-rooms, harness-rooms, hay and corn lofts, and washing places." Each of the firm's drays and wagons had a polished brass plate with the name of the brewery engraved on it.

One person who remembers those brewery stables is Reginald Markham, a retired brewery worker who lives in 14 Auckland Road, one of a group of six houses built by the Star Brewery for its workers in 1891. These houses were called Armstrong Cottages after Mr Charles Armstrong, who ran the brewery. They were first numbered 1–6 Auckland Cottages, but by 1907 they were listed as 10–15 Auckland Road. For many years they were occupied by brewers' draymen, brewers' labourers, maltsters and horsekeepers. Reginald Markham worked for the Star Brewery for 50 years. During the war, he said, the Maltings were used as the local morgue. The Markhams have lived in Auckland Road for 36 years, but Mrs Edith Bareford has been there even longer. Her father, Percy Henry Jarvis, who was a tailor, moved into 8 Auckland Road just before 1915. Edith Bareford was born and brought up there. She went to school in Auckland Road at the Brunswick Council Schools between the Star Brewery Malthouses and the stables and coach house. (Since the 1930s those school buildings have been used as a City health centre and clinic.)

The Barefords and the Markhams have something else in common. They have both held special parties at the social club in Auckland Road, formerly the City Surveyor's Club, now the Yasume Club for Far Eastern Prisoners of War. Edith and Basil Bareford held their wedding reception at the club, Mabel and Reginald Markham celebrated their silver wedding there. I was taken into the Yasume Club (the name means "rest" in Japanese) the other evening by Alfred Bavey, an ex-POW who was a private in the 2nd Cambridgeshires when he was captured in Singapore in 1942. "I was taken to work on the Burma Railway and then shipped on to Japan to work down a coal mine. I was down that mine 30 miles from Hiroshima the day the Atom bomb was dropped," he said. The explosion caused the mine to cave in and Alfred Bavey and several fellow prisoners were trapped down there, badly, and in some cases fatally, injured until they were rescued by other prisoners. The Yasume Club, which has 200 members, started in Auckland Road five years ago, after moving from the Joint Services Club in Coldham's Lane.

The club's president is Don Few of Elsworth, who was a prisoner of the Japanese, working in appalling conditions on the Burma/Siam border building the Merguie Road, where hundreds of men died of disease, malnutrition and torture. "Only 140 out of an original group of 1,700 survived," he said. Among the diseases contracted by the POWs was a wasting illness caused by the parasite *strongaloydies* entering the blood system via bare feet. It is only in the past two years that this parasite has been identified, and many sufferers hitherto unaware of what was causing their lassitude, and the destructive weals on their skin, have been cured at hospitals throughout the country, the local hospital in this area being RAF Ely. Don Few is the FEPOW (Far East Prisoners of War) welfare officer for East Anglia and accompanies all ex-POWs on check-up visits to Ely. Gatherings several times a week at the Yasume Club are not morbid occasions. It is rare for the members to dig up the past and dwell on the "Railway of Death", as they called the Burma railway. Instead the get-togethers are very sociable with bingo, billiards and a drink. It could be said that the Yasume is the focal point of social life in Auckland Road.

As for the New Zealand association implied in the name of Auckland Road, a clue is provided by Marjorie Loakes of Queen Edith's Way, whose mother had relatives in the road. Her mother's uncle David Apthorpe and his cousin Amelia emigrated to Auckland and Amelia, on her return, gave the terrace its name, according to family recollection.

3 Maid's Causeway

10–17 May 1984

Maid's Causeway, Doll's Close . . . what engaging names for a key street. Where do these names come from? Local legend connects the maids of the Causeway (authorities differ on where the apostrophe should go) with the inhabitants of the almshouses built in 1647–8 by Elizabeth Knight at the end of King Street. (Of Doll's Close more in a moment.) But Catherine Hall, the archivist of Gonville and Caius College, disposes of this theory in her article in the *Cambridge Civic Society Newsletter* about the street. She says that it was called the

Causeway in 1634, 18 years *before* the Knight and Mortlock almshouses were built. Mrs Hall's theory is that the maids were dairymaids and countrywomen of all ages coming into town to work, or to the market from the suburb of Barnwell or beyond. She thinks it is more probable that the Causeway, built with money left for that purpose in his will by Stephen Perse, existed mainly for the benefit of the aged poor of the town "toiling up the hill away from the amenities of shops, market and parish church".

Stephen Perse, of Gonville and Caius, who

'Distinctive and handsome' houses in Charles Humfrey's Doll's Close, Maid's Causeway

OPPOSITE: *Room with a view – the roofline of Doll's Close from an attic window of 18 Maid's Causeway*

Richard and Madge Levente with two of their cats, George and Tavie

founded the Perse Grammar School, decided to improve the road in an area that was traditionally "low-lying, miry and foul". Until the end of the 18th century it was where the town of Cambridge came to an end. He said: "I will that my executors and the survivor of them shall within three years next after my decease make a sufficient Causeway from the further end of Jesus Lane to the other end of Barnwell and from the further end of Barnwell to Quy Causeway called Doctor Harvey's Causeway." The Perse Trust paid a roadmender to tackle the section of road nearest the town, and in particular the slope – that railed-off, paved footing – between the end of the town and the Barnwell suburb.

The suburb had been slowly pushing out along the road from Cambridge, but building development on any scale was not possible until after the Enclosure Act relating to Barnwell Fields (1806–7). By 1815 a number of new houses had been built, both at the top of the slope on the Brunswick side, and lower down on the right-hand side. The town's improvement commissioners moved in and noted in September and October 1815 that it was important to improve the crossing over Butt Green and to make a gate to keep the cattle in. The gate then was at the

bottom of Fair Street. Paving and lighting also began, for in December 1815 there were orders for four additional lamps, one at the near end of Jesus Lane, one at the crossing at the foot of Maid's Causeway, and two additional lamps on the new causeway "opposite Mr Burleigh's House". Maid's Causeway was springing to life.

This was the time when Charles Humfrey came on the scene (for some details of his career, see Willow Walk, Orchard Street and Parker Street). In 1810 he acquired Doll's Close, on which he built Willow Walk, Fair Street, Short Street and the houses considered to be the *crème de la crème* of Maid's Causeway. That was just after the enclosure award. Doll was probably a local worthy who farmed that land or at any rate laid claim to it. The site was originally a one-acre enclosed field bordering the medieval open fields. By the end of the 18th century it was in the ownership of the Corporation, and in 1798 they agreed to lease it to the trustees of the late Sir George Downing as the site for their new college. The first clause of the foundation charter of Downing College states the plan "that in and upon Doll's Close there should and might be erected and established one perpetual college . . .". But more grandiose, classical building plans soon meant that the site in Doll's Close was too small. In 1801 the trustees obtained the royal assent to move to Pembroke Leys, where the college was later built. Pembroke Leys, of course, is a huge site and there is room there for further building schemes today. A design by the architect Quinlan Terry, who does wonders reviving the classical orders, is under consideration by Downing at the moment.

After Downing backed out of Doll's Close, it was advertised for sale and snapped up by Humfrey. The scheme he drew up for it consisted of 39 houses, nos. 4–20 on the south side of Maid's Causeway and the houses in Willow Walk, Fair Street and Short Street – a harmonious plan. The principal houses on the site, to quote the Royal Commission on Historical Monuments, were those in Maid's Causeway: "Overlooking Butt Green these consist of five large detached, and two pairs of semi-detached houses set well back from the road, symmetrically disposed, uniform in design and linked by straight screen walls. The houses were built 37 ft wide on plots 46 ft wide." They are distinguished and handsome houses. The Royal Commission explains that in November 1815 Humfrey promised to offer for sale in the spring of 1816 "skeleton shells" and "sites" of houses here. "In 1816 one of the houses was advertised as newly erected and unfinished. They were usually sold on 40-year leases, with Humfrey retaining the freehold. After raising a mortgage of

Regency houses on the north side of Maid's Causeway

£7,000 on Doll's Close in 1842, he was obliged to sell out in 1846."

Some of those Doll's Close houses in Maid's Causeway came up for sale at an auction on Tuesday, 21 August 1849. The catalogue refers *inter alia* to "a capital detached dwelling house, most excellent residences and a very convenient dwelling house, No 1 situate at the corner of Fair Street and the Maid's Causeway, as now in the occupation of Mr Ashman, at a rent of £20". Another house (before renumbering it was no. 5) was a "most excellent family residence". The catalogue describes it as containing "three Sitting Rooms and large Waiting Hall, three Bed Rooms, Bath Room, and two Attics: the Domestic Apartments are most complete, with Yard and Gardens and back entrance with neat Portico in front. This lot is in lease to the Misses Deighton for 40 years, from Lady-day, 1826 . . . and is now in the occupation of Mr Buller."

One of the best-known occupants of Doll's Close in Victorian times was Henry Thomas Hall, an important public figure and local alderman. Born in Cambridge in 1823, he was apprenticed to a printer and worked for several years as a compositor. During his youth he was a great advocate of workers' rights and was a supporter of the Chartists, joining them on marches to London. He spoke at many meetings during the agitation over the Corn Laws. A cultural man, he had a great love of the theatre and was a prominent member of the Cambridge Amateur Dramatic Company. He is best remembered for his contribution to the cause of better education and for his involvement with the Cambridge Free Library. His obituary in the *University Journal, Isle of Ely Herald and Huntingdonshire Gazette* of 20 July 1894, says that he gave time and money "without stint" to promote the library's success, donating 4,297 volumes to its shelves during his lifetime. He was also connected with the Volunteer Movement and was the first Captain of the Fire Brigade. He was mourned at his death as a man who had contributed generously to many aspects of local affairs. "Harry" Hall, as he was known, lived at what was then 1 Maid's Causeway, the house in Doll's Close at the junction with Short Street. No. 2, next door, was the home of Mr William Eaden Lilley, nephew of William Eaden, the joint founder of the firm of Eaden Lilley. The 1871 census describes him as a draper's assistant.

Mrs Margaret Laing of no. 10 tells me that no. 12 used to belong to Mr Barker of Barker and Wadsworth, the mineral water bottlers of Willis Road, and prior to that it was a school. In late Victorian times, there were a great many children living in Doll's Close. It was the age of the large family. The 1871 census shows that two nurses in nos. 7 and 8 between them looked after 13 children. These are after all large family houses, each with two reception rooms on the ground floor, but the layout of the rooms varies, depending on the position of the houses in Doll's Close.

Mrs Margaret Reiss of 18 Maid's Causeway put it like this: "There is a solid house at each end that is two rooms deep, while the houses in the middle are two rooms wide." Dr Bernard Reiss and his wife Margaret, a former independent councillor, have lived in Maid's Causeway for 23 years. They bought the house from an undergraduate who had filled it with lots of students. The Reiss family have gone to great trouble restoring the house – the initial renovations included making safe a stairway down to the basement and kitchen, and removing thousands of nails from floorboards in the large hall where generations of occupants had tacked down carpets and linoleum.

Dr Reiss' middle name is Butts (no connection with Butt Green opposite – the tie-up there is with archery). Among his Butts ancestors was Sir William Butts, MD, a Caius man, who was physician to Henry VIII. A collateral ancestor was Sir Henry Butts, DD, Master of Corpus Christi College and Vice-Chancellor in 1630 at a time when a plague-like pestilence was causing the death of many people in Cambridge. A paternalistic man, Sir Henry was concerned about the suffering of the sick and the poor. In a letter to Lord Coventry, he said there were 5,000 poor and not above 100 who could assist or relieve them. The letter adds: "We have built 40 booths in a remote place upon our commons, whither we forthwith remove those that are infected, where we have placed a German physician who visits them day and night." The inhabitants of the neighbouring villages were afraid to come into Cambridge, so "there is danger of famine as well as of the plague". Distress and inability to help on the scale needed drove Sir Henry to commit suicide. An interesting but very sad comment on the relationship between town and gown.

No. 8, the home since 1968 of Richard and Madge Levente, is one of the houses in Doll's Close which has been least altered over the years. Many of the original fittings are still there – decorated stair treads, fireplaces, and what Richard Levente describes as something like a priest's hole in the basement. A long recess leading off the drawing room, now a convenient storage spot, would originally have housed the commode. Those were the days before sewage systems. Instead of pipes, you relied instead on the night soil cart . . . But from commodes to chandeliers . . . A chandelier twinkling at night reflects in the mirror of the Leventes' drawing room countless images of itself – like a miniature feature of Schönbrunn, says Richard Levente, who is Austrian. A retired RAF Wing Commander, he worked for 14 years as senior technical officer at the Mullard Observatory at Lord's Bridge, literally keeping the radio telescope on the rails.

The views from these Doll's Close drawing rooms across Butt Green to Midsummer Common are the next best thing to having your own country park. If only the cars would somehow disappear, and peacocks could strut there instead. It is this view that Freddie Webber will miss when he moves from 22 Maid's Causeway, otherwise known as 1 Fair Street, to a flat in Tenison Road this week. He and his late wife bought the house ("the recessed wall arch caught my fancy") in 1965. A retired engineer, Mr Webber in his own way is a distinguished resident. In Cambridge rowing circles he is a legendary figure – an oarsman whose rowing career spanned more than half a century, from 1919 to 1976. He has been a member of the Thames Rowing Club at Putney, one of the two great Metropolitan clubs, since 1920. "I am its second oldest member." He joined the Imperial College Eight in the early 1920s. Now Mr Webber from his corner at the junction of Fair Street and Maid's Causeway sees the world pass by, listening to the pigeons in the trees and watching the comings and goings – the fairs, the circuses, the festive occasions on Midsummer Common. All of which make up a permanent moving picture for the residents in Doll's Close, the royal box of Maid's Causeway.

Away now from Charles Humfrey's late Georgian urban housing estate to the north side of Maid's Causeway and the individual Regency houses between Butt Green and the former vicarage of St Andrew the Less, built on land called "Wolfe's Field". This was given to Peterhouse in 1540 by Elizabeth Wolfe, wife of a Cambridge brewer. Peterhouse has a commemorative portrait of her in her widow's weeds. The "modern" estate – that stylish row of Regency houses, each one a little different – is the result of the Barnwell enclosure award of 1811. In 1820–1, the college leased out the land on building leases to leasees who included men called Blacklee, Apthorpe, Brett, Papworth and Sherwin. "Some of the leases gave them permission to build more than one house," said the Peterhouse archivist, Roger Lovatt. The houses remained in the college's possession until 1926, when they sold two of them for a few hundred pounds. After a long gap, the rest were sold between 1950 and 1970. The reason given for the college's parting with them is that they had become affected by the growth of traffic along the Newmarket Road, and their up-keep had become costly. With no strong impulse to keep them, they were sold to the tenants. This is a fairly standard pattern in Cambridge, with colleges acquiring land early on, then developing it after the Enclosure Act, and finally selling it in recent years when there may no longer be the need for accom-modation away from the immediate vicinity of the college. (Many of the Peterhouse houses on Maid's Causeway were hostel-run by landladies for Peter-house undergraduates in the years before they were sold.)

A very fashionable area of Cambridge in which to live, Maid's Causeway (the local vernacular refers to "The Causeway") is now, dare I say, the Islington of the City. At one time, however, it was distinctly unfashionable. Sporting two brothels, it had a par-ticularly bad reputation during the second world war. Four Lamps roundabout, at the end of The

'Gracious, gentrified' houses on the south side of Maid's Causeway

Causeway, was the spot where American Air Force buses used to pick up returning Air Force personnel before taking them back to camp. The airmen could always be sure, apparently, of a jolly send-off, as well as a jolly welcome. Locals at the time used to call Four Lamps "Rainbow Corner". Maintaining vestiges of gentility, Maid's Causeway continued basically as a tough street with a "red light" repu-tation until the late 1960s, says Dr Lisa Jardine, who lives in a handsome double-fronted house, no. 53, which was restored and modernised by Kit Martin, son of Sir Leslie Martin, in 1970. The enormously spacious drawing room of no. 53, now the venue for Lisa Jardine's English seminars and supervisions (she is a Fellow of Jesus College), recalls the Jane Austen era of entertaining and social intrigue.

It was in the 1960s and 1970s that young families took on the job of putting The Causeway back to rights. Full of children who whizzed round to see each other on skateboards before going off to play safely on the green at the back, it became a com-munity street. The Maid's Causeway Residents' Association which sprang into life later on, to fight the Kite development, was led by a mixed group of young professional people, who found the energy to take on the City Council, Grosvenor Estates and

Grafton House in its heyday, when it was the home and surgery of the late Dr H. F. Apthorpe Webb

Jesus College, as well as the strength to refurbish their houses.

One person who has watched the battles, as well as the gentrification, taking place is Mrs Jane Roth, who came to live in Maid's Causeway with her husband, the late George Kingsley Roth, in 1957. When they first bought their house, friends raised their eyebrows at their choice of location, but now of course, as Mrs Roth says, the street has changed. One reason is that it is so central. With the advent of the Grafton Centre, residents are within walking distance of two shopping centres. And while it is a street of double yellow lines, quite a few of the houses on the north side have garages. The Roths came to Maid's Causeway from Fiji, where they had lived since 1942. "My husband was in the colonial administrative services in Fiji, before that we had spent two years in Zanzibar." Jane Roth preferred the Pacific. "Fiji has a very healthy climate for the Tropics." Her husband spoke the language of Fiji, an Oceania language which was first put into print by missionaries. When he retired and they came to Cambridge, he was made honorary keeper of the

Fiji Collection in the Museum of Archaeology and Anthropology established by Baron von Hügel. Jane Roth is carrying on her husband's work: she is editing the diary kept by von Hügel when he went to Fiji in 1874 as a youth of 20. "He spent nearly three years there and kept a very detailed diary recording his impressions of the islands, as well as his adventures and friendships." Parson Kilvert of the South Pacific! Von Hügel donated his Fijian collection to the 'Ark'. Experts consider it one of the finest in the museum. Avid readers of travel books, and I don't mean the Michelin Guides to three-star luxury in France, but rather the adventures of men like Laurens van der Post and Peter Fleming, will be familiar with the name of the pioneer Victorian explorer, Mary Kingsley. There is a tie-up with Kingsley Roth. His father was a museum curator who corresponded with Mary Kingsley, and named his son after her.

But back from Fiji to look at one of the most stately houses in The Causeway. Formerly the vicarage of St Andrew the Less (St Andrew is the 13th-century Abbey Church in Newmarket Road), 73 Maid's Causeway is now a private house. Built in 1830 – it is Grade 2 "listed" – of Cambridge hand-made bricks, it was substantially altered in the

1890s, when the then incumbent, called Sibson, added two big rooms on the right hand side, giving the vicarage a big drawing room. Canon Edward Church, whose sons went out as missionaries to Ruanda, is remembered for all the activities that he promoted at the vicarage – the Boys' Brigade used to meet regularly on the lawn. The authentic-looking porch is not an original feature of the house. It is a becoming addition which the present owner, Dr Gordon Simpson (who bought the house in 1960 and reroofed and renovated it), acquired from a rectory in Bookham, Surrey, where it was advertised for sale. The present vicarage of St Andrew the

Less and Christchurch was built in the garden of no. 73. No. 71 next door was probably the curate's house.

The other stately house in Maid's Causeway is Grafton House, built in 1830 complete with stables in extensive grounds. For at least 30 years it was the home of an insurance agent, William Waters, who moved there from Jesus Lane in 1854. It was the next owner, Benjamin Jolley, who developed Grafton House's garden frontage on Maid's Causeway by building some solid Victorian houses there which blend uneasily into the Regency Causeway. These six houses have names like Hazelwood, Oak Hurst and Conway House, reflecting the rustic aspirations of the Victorians.

The site of the Zebra public house in the 1920s

Another house in this stretch of The Causeway, which was formerly called Brunswick Place, has a famous theatrical association. North House, no. 66, a detached dwelling at the gate of Grafton House, was once lived in by the actor and film star Robert Donat, and his wife, Ella Voysey. Both were acting at the Festival Theatre in Newmarket Road in, among other productions, *The Rivals*. Their "ideal digs" in Maid's Causeway, to quote Ella Voysey, was their first married home: they arrived there in September 1929, after their wedding and honeymoon in August. J.C. Trewin's biography of Robert Donat cites a family letter from Ella: "We have two large rooms. The sitting-room with plain cream walls on which we have hung the etchings given us for our wedding present." They sat on velvet cushions on leather-covered brown furniture. Mrs C. D. Newman of Crathern Way was 14 when the Donats came to North House, which was owned then by her parents, Mr and Mrs Smee. She writes that "Robert Donat, in fact, took his first screen test while living with us, and I can remember how anxious he was in case his asthma proved troublesome on the day . . . one of his favourite dishes was plaice and chips, and he was also very fond of apple charlotte 'as only Mrs Smee can cook it'. Many now famous names passed through the door of no. 66 – the producer Tyrone Guthrie and Flora Robson, to name but two. My parents lived there until 1938, when they became licensees of the Rhadegund Tap in James Street." No. 66 is now up for sale.

Mrs Kathleen Apthorpe Webb, whose father-in-law, Frederick Apthorpe Webb, bought Grafton House from Benjamin Jolley, remembers the Donat connection with Maid's Causeway. She was living in Grafton House then – it was her home with her late husband Dr Hugh Apthorpe Webb for more than 50 years. At one time they were the only family in The Causeway with a car. It was then a street of bicycles; also a street of railings, many of which came down in the war, together with the gates of Grafton House, which were removed without warning. A sandblasted Grafton House is now the headquarters and offices of the Grafton Centre's architects, who work in open-plan style in the interior of a house that for many years saw happy family life. It is still, however, one of the landmarks of Maid's Causeway.

Before the development of the Grafton House frontage, there was a row of little shops and houses between Grafton House and James Street, where the Zebra public house was rebuilt in the 1930s. In 1867, there were two beer retailers there (later the William and Mary and the Zebra) and there were shops too; a grocer, a greengrocer and a milliner and dressmaker at no. 30a (old numbering), Miss Elizabeth Robinson. Causeway Court, later Causeway Passage, between nos. 50 and 52, was once a little artisans' enclave – a sweep, coal porter, painter, groom, baker and sugar boiler all lived there in 1884. Between Grafton House and Causeway Court was Eden Lodge (no. 54), built in 1874 by the local firm of Thoday's as the manse for the Eden Baptist Chapel round the corner. Many of the tall gracious houses, now extensively gentrified, some with sitting rooms on the first floor, which descend the slope of The Causeway to Fair Street, were in Victorian times run as lodging houses. In the 1920s and 1930s, the houses, some of which have names like St Jude's, Long View and Brindisi (no. 36), were the homes of bakers, an engine driver, a gardener and a grocer's manager. Today the owners are professional people such as architects and bankers; and Sir Clive Sinclair once lived at Brunswick Lodge.

4 Willow Walk

29 December 1983 – 12 January 1984

On 6 April 1821 an advertisement in the *Cambridge Chronicle*, for the sale of the lease of two houses in Willow Walk, described them as being in that "generally admired spot Willow Walk, so judiciously allowed for pleasantness, salubrity of the air, and uniformity of building as well as for the extensive views they command (with an almost sure prospect of not being built before) to be unrivalled in the town".

When the houses in Willow Walk – the earliest

symmetrical terrace in Cambridge – were first built in 1815 they were indeed in open country. Neither New Square nor Jesus Lane had been built up, and building had hardly begun in Maid's Causeway. The tradesmen, clerks and college servants who were among the original occupiers lived in a rural setting. They would have looked from their windows out across the fields to Emmanuel College, and could well have considered themselves country dwellers . . . well, almost. Those rolling views lasted for less than 20 years – in 1834–5 the north terrace of New Square was built.

A private, still unmade road included in the Cam-

Houses in Willow Walk, the earliest symmetrical terrace in Cambridge

bridge No. 1 Conservation Area in 1969, Willow Walk is part of the famous Doll's Close, the small development halfway between the old centre of Cambridge and the surburb of Barnwell (see Maid's Causeway). The architect, Charles Humfrey (1772–1848), whose brother owned the mill from which Mill Road gets its name, was the son of a local carpenter and builder. Charles trained as an architect in London at the Royal Academy Schools; he was a pupil of the neo-classicist James Wyatt, R.A., Surveyor General and Controller of Works. Architectural historians note that Humfrey, who practised as an architect in Cambridge carrying out speculative developments, probably treated Doll's Close as his first venture of this kind. Regency building is rather precious in Cambridge because there is so little of it. The editor of the *Victoria County History*, Mr A.P. Baggs, who used to live at 9 Willow Walk, which he rescued from demolition, says that Humfrey's design in Doll's Close was for two symmetrical terraces, one facing Maid's Causeway and having detached and semi-detached houses in externally identical blocks joined by low walls, and the other, facing Willow Walk, being a low terrace accentuated by a central pediment and terminal wings. The outward-facing square was completed by more small houses which have end elevations designed as pavilions, beyond the ends of the terraces.

How does Willow Walk get its name? It is thought to be an old descriptive name for a footpath which followed a ditch along the edge of the Doll's Close field. The suggestion that willow trees grew in the road until the 20th century is attractive, but there are in fact no trees marked on early maps.

Humfrey kept the freehold of all the houses in Willow Walk but sold 40-year leases on all but nos. 2, 3, 4, 9 and 10, which were let at rents of between £12 and £8 per year. For a while no. 10 was a public baths. The *Cambridge Chronicle* for 11 August 1820 announced that "the Public Baths no. 10 [Willow Walk], which have been long in preparation, will be opened on Monday next, the 14th. Terms for warm or cold bathing may be known by applying to Mr Carter on the premises." As well as being an architect, Charles Humfrey was an entrepreneur. He was a banker as well as a man of property, and a combative member of the Corporation. In 1837 he was mayor. But his financial dealings were sometimes unsuccessful, and after raising a mortgage on Doll's Close in 1842, he was obliged to sell the freehold in 1846. His Willow Walk houses, which fit together like a jigsaw, were sold off as pairs for investment

Gas lamp in Willow Walk

rather than for occupation, a pattern of ownership which persisted into the present century.

Five years later the 1851 census shows the pattern of ownership in Willow Walk. No. 1, which in 1830 had been a school, was the home of a retired surgeon called Charles Dyer. He lived there with his wife, son, daughter and two servants. William Lofts, a college servant, fitted into no. 2 with his wife, three sons and three daughters. A clerk, Thomas Cole, and his wife and servant, lived at no. 3. Thomas Colston, a tailor, was at no. 4; he had two lodgers, probably undergraduates. William Thirkettle, a solicitor's managing clerk, and his wife, son and daughter and their servant occupied no. 5. Joseph Mansfield, listed there in 1846, lived at no. 6 with his daughter and three lodgers. More undergraduates? He was a retired merchant's carter. William Hunt, an auctioneer's clerk, his wife and a lodger lived at no. 7. Susannah Jarrold, a retired grocer, and her son and daughter were at no. 8. Matthew Allis, listed as bookseller and bathkeeper, lived at no. 9 with his wife, daughter and servant, which suggests that the houses had been renumbered at some time, for it was no. 10 that was advertised as the bath house in the *Cambridge Chronicle* in 1821 – but in 1851 Fanny Vials and her son and two daughters lived at no. 10, which together with no. 9 formed the central pediment of Humfrey's design. Three annuitants (they were in receipt of annuities) lived at nos. 11, 12 and 13 with relatives. There were, starting at no. 11, Sarah Cullington, Elizabeth Poole and Mary Youngman. Thomas Cross, listed as unemployed, lived at no. 14 with his wife, four sons and a daughter. Mary Barrett, a landed town proprietor, owned no. 15. She lived there with three sons, a daughter and a servant. David Rootham at no. 16 was a lay clerk and carpenter; William Lusher at no. 17 a builder; and William Smith at no. 18 a proprietor of horses, who had been living in Willow Walk since 1837.

When Humfrey designed Willow Walk he left space between the ends of the main neo-classical terrace and the corner buildings to Short Street and Fair Street. The space was used as gardens. It was towards the end of the 19th century that these gardens were built over. At the Short Street end the building was probably for William Port, the cab proprietor, who lived in no. 1, and at the other end next to no. 17 it was for extensions to the Willow Tree public house, first listed in street directories in 1866. In the 1880s the name of Scales appears in the directories in connection with the Willow Tree pub, signifying that it was run by Mr Scales of Scales Brewery, now the Cambridge Arms public house in King Street. We know that the gardens at the ends of Willow Walk had gone by 1886 when the first

large-scale Ordnance Survey map of this area was made. Strips of garden between the pavement and the roadway at the east end of the street had disappeared as well, although they remained at the west end. The gardens then coincided with the length of roadway which was enclosed by gates outside nos. 1 and 9. Local tradition has it that these wooden gates were removed during the first world war by billeted soldiers seeking firewood, but the privacy of the right of way was protected by notices under the 1922 Act. Soon after the second world war the hinged shutters which had framed each ground-floor window were removed from most of the houses, probably to reduce the cost of external painting. All the shutters, once original features of the houses in Willow Walk, have now unfortunately disappeared.

During the late 1950s and early 1960s the future of the houses was threatened both by a road scheme and by slum clearance, a spectre which hung over several parts of Cambridge at that time, the precious Little St Mary's Lane being a case in point. Officers in the Health Department at that time were particularly zealous. When Tony Baggs bought 9 Willow Walk in 1964, the house was condemned as "unfit for human habitation" and the whole road was bracing itself for a "Mitcham's Corner" type extension of Four Lamps which would have left the Maid's Causeway houses on the traffic island. How sacrilegious that would have been! Eighteen months before, Ian Fleming (not the author of James Bond) had bought no. 3. About six months after that John Morton bought no. 13, now the home of Dorothy Silberston. Mrs Silberston is on the national council of the Schizophrenia Fellowship, a charity which raises money to help people with specific problems arising from this illness. They were the first three purchasers who extensively restored and modernised their houses, operations which included digging out the floor of the basement to get a ceiling height which satisfied the health regulations (the ceilings were originally 6 ft). They all bought their houses for less than £1,000, and a year or so after Tony Baggs moved in, he was offered nos. 7 and 8 with sitting tenants for £1,100 the pair. But, he says, he didn't have "any spare money or any real inclination to get into property". In the 1960s Frank and Dorothy King lived at no. 8. He was an Irish builder whose gang dug out the channels for the water pipes in the Bòtanic Garden. Dorothy King made gowns for Joshua Taylor.

Older residents remember the Misses Curzon, two sisters who had lived in the road at no. 10 (the former bath house) since their childhood. They were excellent neighbours. At one time they kept a small haberdashery shop on the Fair Street corner. The large plate-glass window of the shop is now incorporated into the Church Army Hostel. No. 10 is now the home of Robin and Jenny Anderson, who bought it in 1967 for £2,500. Robin Anderson, a freelance computer specialist and typesetter, had to do a lot of work in the basement of the house to satisfy health regulations. He and his wife made one big room out of six very small ones, including little pantries and larders, whose walls of plaster and lath were rotting. During the renovations the Andersons discovered that they shared a well with no. 9, and at the end of their garden they found the original earth closet (which pre-dates all living memory). The house also had an outside lavatory, so it was quite a museum of plumbing.

The process of gentrification continues in Willow Walk. Ian Fleming and Mary Bernard of no. 3 acquired no. 4 three years ago; they have gutted the interior and amalgamated the two houses. No. 14 was converted for King's don Nick Humfreys about 12 years ago. He sold the house to a chess grand-

master. The earliest symmetrical terrace in Cambridge, in 1973 Willow Walk was listed in the statutory list of buildings of architectural and historic interest. Quite an achievement for the conservationists who rescued it from slum clearance.

Mention the name of the street to most Cambridge people and they will say like a chorus of Pavlov's dogs, "Willow Walk – that's where the vet used to be." The veterinary surgeons were Kirkbride, Carter and Robins, now in Chesterton Road. They were in practise at no. 12 for 12 years (1961–73), during which time they can be said to have put Willow Walk on the map. It was a popular practice ("James Herriot" in the Kite!), and the fears of elderly residents about the sort of animals that might turn up there were soon allayed, although once a horsebox was squeezed into the road – "Just a routine innoculation, but they decided to come to us," said Mr Kirkbride.

For many years Willow Walk has been a private road whose gates are locked at night, where genteel retired people have co-existed with the skilled entrepreneurs who have manned the ends of the road, as it were. There is a garage at either end of Willow Walk; no. 1 is the Short Street Garage, first

Mr Frank Bush at his garage in Willow Walk

established there in 1948, while the Bush family at the Fair Street end have been in business there since 1919. Before it became a garage and filling station no. 1 was owned by cab proprietors. In 1914 the street directory lists William Bradford as the motor cab proprietor. In 1884 it was William Port. But before cabs were installed there, no. 1, according to the 1841 census return, was a school. Before Frank Bush's father Arthur established his garage in Willow Walk, on a lease from Jesus College, the premises belonged to the cab proprietor Philip Nightingale, who in 1895 was living at 7 Willow Walk. He kept his hansom cabs in the stable and shed which became Bush's garage.

Willow Walk used to be inhabited by skilled artisans. Between 1874 and 1904, when the Church Army Labour Home was first listed at no. 19 (it was listed in Fair Street in 1901), the houses in Willow Walk were occupied by cabinet makers, college laundresses, tailors, ironmongers, stonemasons, whitesmiths, carpenters, lodging house keepers, hairdressers, college servants, solicitors' clerks, cooks, bedmakers, builders and photographers. And Willow Walk in 1898 had its resident school attendance officer – a sign of the times? One imagines that many of the artisans found work in those parts of Cambridge, where there was a building boom in the last years of Queen Victoria's reign, particularly in Sturton Town, and in the railway township of Romsey, where the green fields of Barnwell were developed as building land.

No one has lived in Willow Walk longer than Mrs Edna ("Ned") O'Connell, who works as practice manager for a group of local doctors. She moved into 5 Willow Walk in 1950 with her young family. They had been bombed out of London during the war. Who were the inhabitants then? "When I first came here they seemed to be very old widows," she said. "But as the old people died, the houses were bought by young dons who then began to modernise them." The process is now being reversed, and as houses come on the market they are bought by retired people, such as Sir Henry and Lady Lintott (Sir Henry is the retired British High Commissioner for Canada), and Dr and Mrs John Hodgkin, who bought no. 9 from Tony Baggs. Dr Hodgkin is an

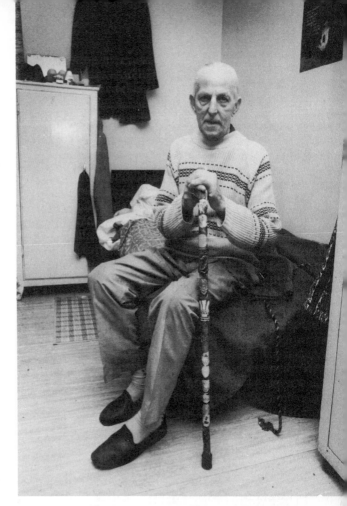

The oldest resident at the Church Army Hostel in Willow Walk, Mr Harold Clarke. He was born in Peterborough in 1901, and spent his 21st birthday in India. The hostel, for over 30 men who would otherwise be homeless, was built on the site of the Willow Tree public house early in the century

artist whose abstract work is influenced by the paintings of the French artists Claude Lorraine and Georges Rouault. Local artists might well be inspired by the sight of the grass growing again on New Square, a phenomenon that can be observed from Willow Walk bedrooms, and a reminder of days of former rusticity.

5 Orchard Street

26 April–3 May 1984

Orchard Street, Cambridge's best-known chocolate box of a street, is to be found, perhaps appropriately, on the edge of what used to be called the Garden of Eden (see Eden Street). Not *quite* an Earthly Paradise for those living there now, Orchard Street, and in particular the famous cottages with the "bungalow look" on the north side, still has enough of an aesthetic appeal to excite architectural historians, and those who value domestic buildings in a city where there is precious little of domestic interest to write home about.

The cottages on the north side were built in 1825,

probably for his own servants, by the architect Charles Humfrey (see Willow Walk). In his thesis on Humfrey, David Chaffin explains that in 1809 Humfrey had purchased four acres between Parker's Piece and Christ's Pieces, as subsequently set out in the 1811 enclosure award, from James Burleigh. On this estate, called St Andrew's Close, he built in 1816 "a capital mansion house in the Elizabethan style". He then extended his estate by leasing Brewer's Piece, two acres adjoining to the west,

OPPOSITE: *Architect, builder and banker Charles Humfrey. From a portrait in the possession of Mrs Martha German of Emmanuel Road*

Orchard Street in August 1938; it is still much the same

Mrs Gladys Cable with her porcelain cat "Bobby"

with Stores, Coppers, Shelves, etc., and in the most convenient manner. All the Gardens are separated from one another, and the fronts of the houses are all alike. Each house is amply supplied with excellent spring water." The advertisement of the auction, which was to be held at the Red Lion Inn, Petty Cury, at 7 o'clock in the evening, also referred to three lots of building ground for sale adjoining the houses.

"Orchard Street," continued the announcement, "is now a public thoroughfare (but for foot passengers only); there has been put down recently a neat and substantial bricked and pebbled foot-path along the whole front (which is uniform), and there is an underground barrel-drain from end to end of the Street, communicating with two common sewers. Every house is at present respectably occupied." At that time, and until the cottages were modernised in the 1960s, each cottage was divided into two smaller cottages, numbered (a) and (b). The next auction of Humfrey property was held at the Red Lion on Thursday, 23 October 1845. Six lots referred to houses in Orchard Street. In all 12 Orchard Street houses were still for sale. And then the *Cambridge Chronicle* of 10 April 1847 advertised *inter alia* four houses for sale in Orchard Street, each with a rent of about £8 per annum, and eight lots of building ground in Orchard Street were offered for sale, by the foot, "so that purchasers will not be required to take more than they want".

The notice of auction on 11 June 1845 offered "the whole of Orchard Street, comprising Seventeen substantial brick-and-tile houses". Now as we all know, there are only 13 cottages on the north side of Orchard Street and no. 16 is across the other side of Clarendon Street; what happened was that nos. 14 and 15 were the victims of that very modern phenomenon, a road widening scheme. In 1913 the Town Council went ahead with its scheme to construct a new street connecting Clarendon Street with New Square, and to widen Fair Street. But the scheme had had some opposition. On 10 August 1911, at the Town Council meeting, Councillor Gray moved that "it be an instruction to the Town Clerk not to proceed further with negotiations for the purchase of property required for the construction of a new street connecting Clarendon Street with New Square and the widening of Fair Street". But the mayor stated that the matter had proceeded so far that a resolution on the subject was useless, and ruled the motion out of order.

Miss Ena Mitchell, of Halifax Road, author of *Notes on the History of Parker's Piece*, points out that the present no. 16 has a slightly different design from the remaining 13 in that harmonious curve.

from the owners, Corpus Christi College, and in 1825 he bought Brewer's Piece in exchange for land to the south of Barnwell new church adjoining his brother's mill. (The mill stood at the junction of Mill Road and Covent Garden.) Orchard Street was laid out along the northern boundary of the estate soon afterwards. It is said that Humfrey built the cottages so that they appeared to have only one storey in order to preserve the privacy of his own sumptuous garden – their bedroom windows are at the back and look out towards New Square. When Mrs Kidd moved into no. 38 in 1939, her landlady pointed out a doorway in the garden "leading into the estate, where the workers and people who lived in the little houses went through". There had been a washhouse on one side and a brewery on the other.

It was 20 years later, in 1845, that Humfrey got into difficulties. Several liquidating auctions of his property were held during 1845 and 1847 (see Parker Street). In the *Cambridge Chronicle* of 7 June 1845, a notice of the auction offered "the whole of Orchard Street, comprising Seventeen substantial brick-and-tile houses". The houses, with rents totalling £235 per annum, were, said the advertisement, "in the best possible condition, having been built only about 20 years, each house is fitted

The Golden Rose public house at the junction of Orchard Street and Emmanuel Street (formerly Miller's Lane) in 1912 – it is an architect's office now

She is led to think that, to make the 17 of 1845, there may have been a house, similar to the present no. 16, abutting the present no. 1, on the land now occupied by the Victorian house numbered 18 Emmanuel Road. This "extra" house, she says, would have been opposite the Golden Rose public house, offered at the three auctions mentioned above. Orchard Street in those early days, and well into the 20th century, was the home of local artisans and college servants. In 1881 there was Mrs Annie Ayres, a bedmaker's help, living at no. 5b, while further up at the long-since-demolished no. 15 Ann Howard kept a mangle. Several college servants lived on the opposite side of the road.

You cannot go far in Cambridge without encountering a royal connection. Nipping through Emmanuel College the other day en route to Orchard Street I stumbled on a "dress rehearsal" for the Queen's visit on 16 May. Pristine buildings and an absence of tangled bikes were the pointers. And then on via Emmanuel's "Paddock" (a brilliant "country" route which avoids the fumes and swirling traffic in Emmanuel Road) to Orchard Street, which has its own royal associations. This time it is the Duke of Gloucester. As an undergraduate at Magdalene College in the 1960s he shared a house with fellow undergraduates in Victoria Street. The link with Orchard Street is that Prince Richard, as he then was, was a conscientious chap and patronised the local shop, Percy Wing's at the corner of Clarendon Street and Orchard Street. He appears to have spent much of his time scoffing Ribena lollies there! The Wings remember his popping in, sometimes twice a day, for a cooling lick.

Everyone who lives within a mile of Clarendon and Orchard Streets knows just what an asset Wing's is to the area. It is the gelling agent in the community, the spot where all members of the local, village-like society can get together, pass the time of day, hear the latest news and pick up their groceries. It is the place where elderly people living alone can be sure of the same sort of welcome as the pleasant prince in search of his sweeties. In the case of the elderly they get more than a welcome. Mr Wing and his wife Sylvia actively cosset their elderly customers, going around to help them if necessary. "My husband takes coal to them and chops wood for them," says Mrs Wing. The Wings deliver groceries if people are stuck, and generally strive very hard to maintain the high standards of service established by Percy Wing's father, Percy Wing Snr, who opened his general stores there in about 1910. In earlier times the shop was a public house called the Two Swans, but it became a shop long before the Wings began trading there. The 1881 street directory lists John Clark, a baker and groom, at nos. 17 and 18. As a boy Percy Wing helped his father in the shop, but he worked in the motor trade before taking over in 1947 because of his father's failing health.

One person with a vivid memory of Percy Wing Snr is Mrs Gladys Cable of 24 Orchard Street, who married and came to live there in Dunkirk week in 1940. "I remember Percy Wing's father as a very tall man in a striped apron, a typical grocer he was." Mrs Cable and her late husband first rented and then bought their house from Miss Kathleen Humm, who lived at no. 25. Miss Humm's father, Henry Humm, was a butler; he is listed as such in the street directories of the 1880s. As well as remembering the Humm family, Mrs Cable is able to refer me to her late husband's family. Henry Cable, the well-known baker in Sturton Street (see below), was Mrs Cable's husband's grandfather. More Cambridge connections . . . Musicologists will know the name of the singer Margaret Cable – Mrs Cable's daughter. She is married to John Fletcher, the tuba player in the London Symphony Orchestra. The musical talent runs in the family. Although unable to read music, Mrs Cable has a very special gift – she can play by ear any piece of music that she has heard. I was entertained to an impromptu piano recital of dizzily catching Chopin waltzes and Mozart arias. It was a real cultural treat on that sunny morning in Orchard Street and quite matched the more indulgent pleasure of the Ribena lolly that I licked to keep up with the duke . . .

Miss Marjorie Hopkins, who lives on what we ought to call the over-exposed, showpiece, "listed" side of Orchard Street, also has Cambridge connections. Born in 1903 at 6 Shaftesbury Road, she is the daughter of Jodrell Hopkins, who ran a hunting stables and horse dealing establishment opposite the Fitzwilliam Museum in Trumpington Street. "It was a riding school with up to 60 horses," said Miss Hopkins. Patrons of the establishment included the late Duke of Gloucester and the late Prince Albert (King George VI), who while up at Cambridge used to enjoy playing polo in Long Road every week. Jodrell Hopkins is perhaps better known for his achievements in the canine world: he developed the Norfolk terrier. Known as the Hopkins terrier, this breed was achieved by crossing and recrossing very small, very game Irish with Glen of Imaal terriers. Art historians will be familiar with Gainsborough's portrait of Paul Jodrell. "He was my great-great-grandfather's brother's son," said Miss Hopkins. The famous Gainsborough portrait hangs in the Frick Collection in New York. Miss Hopkins is a retired children's nurse who trained in the Truby King school of child care in Christchurch, New Zealand. She looked after children in New Zealand and Australia. On 18 December 1929, while sailing from Australia to New Zealand, she was shipwrecked off a dangerous stretch of the New Zealand coast with a large number of passengers. "We spent all night in lifeboats, and I held on to a friend's five-month-old baby."

Miss Hopkins is one of the many inhabitants of Orchard Street who value the village-like atmosphere of the area, appreciating its amenities and its proximity to the city centre. In the busy tourist season it is a little oasis amid the roar of traffic, a village street in the centre of a world-famous town.

6 Earl Street

11 August 1983

Earl Street, off Emmanuel Road, a stone's throw from the glorious technicolour flowerbeds of Christ's Pieces, is one of those early Victorian streets in the "care" of the New Square Residents' Association which was built, together with Victoria and Clarendon Streets, on the site of Charles Humfrey's mansion and grounds, between 1846 and 1870. To be precise, Earl Street, and neighbouring Victoria Street, where the present Duke of Glou-

Calligrapher Gertrude Horsley with the roll of honour of Emmanuel College

cester had a house when he was an undergraduate at Magdalene, were built on land occupied by Humfrey's stables, called The Mews on drawings of the period.

There is an attractive harmony about the Earl Street houses, although they vary in size and detail. Some have basements, some don't. Houses without basements appear to qualify for a parking meter outside. Some have attics, and now the inevitable roof room is on the way, as the quest for space hots up in what has become a highly desirable, smart residential area in the City centre. The average price

35

Mrs Beryl Duffus with an oak chest of drawers

time were printers, carpenters, a bookbinder, a whitesmith, a plumber and college servants. The parish clerk of St Andrew the Great, D. Bunting, lived in the street in 1874, as did Thomas Metcalfe, the head porter at St John's College. He lived at no. 19 for several years. By 1904 George Howard, the "boots" at the University Arms Hotel, had moved to 9 Earl Street.

Between the wars most of the Earl Street houses were University lodging houses; being so close to the centre, it was a popular area with undergraduates. Some of the lodging houses would have been run by widows and spinsters glad of an income. Those were the days when undergraduates were, by modern standards, pampered. Mr Leslie Staples, who has lived at 2a Earl Street for 58 years (his mother bought the house in 1925), reminded me that the colleges used to send shoe-blacks round to clean undergraduates' shoes on the doorstep every morning. And special meals would be sent round on silver salvers, perched on trays supported on the servants' heads.

The Staples had undergraduates from Downing College lodging with them. "Two became eminent judges, another is a distinguished skin specialist." Leslie Staples, who came from Soham where his father had worked in the family butchery business established nearly 200 years ago, worked as a clerk with Ryder and Amies for 35 years. For a further ten years he was with James Neal, the tailors at the corner of Silver Street and Trumpington Street. His mother bought the house from Mrs M.B. Chamberlain, who had moved from the area to the south of France. Phyllis and Reginald Roberson, of 2 Earl Street, are also long-established local residents. Reginald Roberson, born at no. 5 in 1909, is the grandson of Walter Roberson, who started a car hire business at no. 3 in the 1890s. He started off hiring horses, then it was cabs and finally private cars. His horses were tethered on the site of no. 2a.

The environment of Earl Street has changed dramatically in recent years. Dons and senior members of the University have made their homes in houses once lodged in by their undergraduates. The atmosphere – in the early 1970s it was seedy – is now rather village-like, and people are very neighbourly. If anyone has a skip outside their front door as part of a building operation, local residents creep out at midnight with their unwanted junk and dump it in the skip, and the chances are that they will all meet there as if in some badly organised raiding party!

Beryl Duffus and her husband Philip, who is a lecturer in immunology at the Veterinary School, have lived at 1 Earl Street for five years. They came

of houses in Earl Street now is more than £50,000; no. 26, the home of Magdalene bursar Denis Murphy, is up for sale at £69,500. Compare that with £554 paid for no. 2a in 1925.

Dons have been tinkering away at the Earl Street houses for the past ten years or so, creating a little Canonbury in an area where the original residents were largely artisans. Back in the 1870s and 1880s Earl Street had two breweries. J.F. Constable was running the Falcon Brewery at no. 1 in 1874. In 1884 Henry Moden, across the road at no. 2, is described in the street directory as a brewer and wine merchant. In the 1870s Earl Street had its own school – the Preparatory Day School at no. 23 run by Miss L. Lister, who would appear to have been the daughter of Edward Lister the tailor. Other residents at that

to Cambridge from Kenya. Mrs Duffus' hobby is collecting and selling antiques, and she runs a small antiques consultancy service from her home, advising people on furniture. She has a stock of waxes and polishes suitable for antique furniture, oak being her favourite wood. Beryl Duffus is quite lyrical about living in Earl Street. "It is like being in your own little village." Percy Wing's grocer's shop on the corner of Orchard Street is the mainstay of the area, and there is a good local baby-sitting circle.

Roger French of no. 13 is another of those dons with an interesting hobby. A medical historian, he is "very well up in cider making and has written a book about the subject," says a neighbour and friend. Artistic skill and talent is also a feature of the Earl Street community. Anna Thorgerson at no. 19 is a potter with a studio in her garden. Gertrude Horsley at no. 29 is a calligrapher of world renown, whose work is exhibited in the Fitzwilliam as well as in numerous private collections. She says that her nicest commission was to design a commonplace book for an American scientist. Gertrude Horsley taught at the Cambridge School of Art (see East Road); among her pupils was Ronald Searle. Michael Barnes, husband of local campaigner Alison Barnes, is an architect. No. 37, now the home of Frank and Maureen Fallside, was imaginatively adapted in 1968 by the American architect Nathan Silver for himself and his wife. Soon after the conversion was completed, the house was featured in *Homes and Gardens* and was opened to the public in aid of the Shelter organisation.

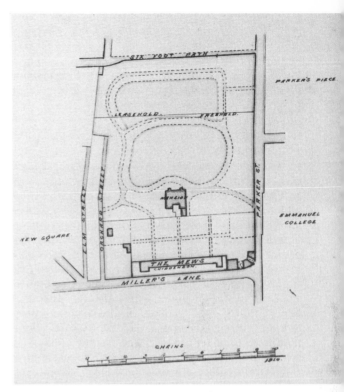

The ground plan of Charles Humfrey's mansion house and grounds dated 1846, showing the layout of adjacent streets

7 Parker Street

31 March–7 April 1983

In 1838 15,000 people sat down to a gargantuan meal on Parker's Piece to celebrate the Coronation of Queen Victoria (see p. 45). It was the year in which building started in nearby Parker Street, where the landowner was the mayor for that year, Charles Humfrey, the architect and banker who had acquired the land between Melbourne Place and Christ's Pieces in 1809. Humfrey built almost entirely for the town rather than the University, although he did a few odd jobs for the colleges like modifying the river front at Clare. His main legacy to Cambridge apart from the Doll's Close development (see Maid's Causeway and Willow Walk) was streets of houses near Parker's Piece, of which nos. 1–6 Parker Street are examples. The entrance to Clarendon House, the large Elizabethan-style mansion he built for himself (see Orchard Street), was from Parker Street, through what is now nos. 7 and 7a. That is the way the carriages would have swept in. In the garden of no. 7a, belonging to Professor Charles Robertson, from Oxford, you can see in the brickwork the archway of the stables. In the garden of 2 Emmanuel Road, home of Mrs Martha German, there is an interesting hexagonal glass gazebo, another relic of the Humfrey estate. It would have been an ornament in Charles Humfrey's garden where, it is said, the family kept pheasants.

Mrs German's great-aunt, Miss Annie Buttery, was housekeeper to the great-grandchildren of Charles Humfrey for 50 years. Their name was Eggleston, and their mother was Humfrey's granddaughter. Humfrey's daughter Sarah married Professor James Cumming, professor of chemistry, in 1820. Martha German acted as companion to her great-aunt when she was frail and poorly. It was

Terraced houses in Parker Street on a quiet morning

Haute cuisine at Emmanuel College with the late chef, Sid Archer

then that she acquired many photographs of the Humfrey family, which she treasures and looks after. The portrait of Charles Humfrey (p. 31) is particularly fine.

In 1846 Humfrey was in desperate financial straits. His political opposition to Mortlock the banker had involved him in considerable expense (Mortlock was part of the corrupt Cambridge Corporation at the time). He had founded a bank, the forerunner of the National Westminster at the corner of Bene't Street and Trumpington Street, and he was involved in banking projects in London. It is said that before 1846, whenever he was short of money, he sold off a bit of his extensive gardens. Nos. 1–6 Parker Street were built on the periphery of those gardens. But on 6 August 1846 his mansion, offices, garden, pleasure grounds and paddock, and the Doll's Close estate – the area bounded by the Newmarket Road, Willow Walk, Short Street and Fair Street – all freehold houses, were sold by auction in London, at Garraway's Coffee House, Cornhill.

The sale particulars gave an illuminating picture of the Humfrey establishment. "The Mansion House is beautifully situate in the centre of its own Grounds. It is in the Elizabethan Style and was erected in the most substantial manner without regard to expense; it is extremely well adapted for the residence of a Banker, Merchant, or Professional Man; or, from the increasing importance of Cambridge, offers an advantageous speculation to the Capitalist for the erection of Villas, &c, from its contiguity to Parker's Piece, which is open and unenclosed ground, and will always remain so." The "walled Garden, newly planted" and the "beautiful Pleasure Grounds with highly ornamental Timber Trees and Shrubs of 30 years growth" would have been a strong selling point. Then there was "a highly ornamental and very productive Paddock adjoining, with Chaise-house, Stable and Poultry Yard, with entrance from Parker's Piece". This paddock was held under a lease from St Peter's College (Peterhouse) for 40 years from Michaelmas, 1836. It was altogether an extensive estate, clearly the stately home of the area.

Architectural historians have said that the terrace formed by nos. 1–6 Parker Street was built in 1838. Their evidence is not a set of deeds, but a brick at the back of no. 5, on which the initials EN and the date 1838 have been scratched. Another clue to a more distant past is to be found in one of two tiny cellars at no. 5. The clue is in the wall, made of large boulders or chunks of clunch which the owners of the house, Marjorie and Sylvia Gage, believe could have come from the Dominican Priory which was formerly on the site of Emmanuel College opposite. When Marjorie and Sylvia Gage look out of their drawing room window what they see of Emmanuel College is the huge red brick Victorian building called The Hostel. The centre part was built in 1885, to the design of W.M. Fawcett, to provide comparatively inexpensive accommodation for undergraduates. Between 1892 and 1894 The Hostel was extended to the north and south by J.L. Pearson, who also built a tutor's house, which adjoined it. "We had always admired the house," said Miss Sylvia Gage. "We used to walk past and watch it being done up, although our mother's reaction was that she could not live right on the street." The house originally had two rooms, one behind the other, to each side of the entrance passage, the width of one of the back rooms being reduced to leave space for a square staircase. In the Gage house the four little front rooms have been made into two large ones. Like the other houses in the terrace it has a small yard at the back enclosed by brick walls. Each house would have had its privy in one corner. The gardens at the back of Parker Street form quite a patchwork.

Nos. 14, 15 and 16 Parker Street were incorporated into Emmanuel College in 1979. Emma bought the houses, built in 1860, from Jesus College, and saved them from demolition. They are now hostels for undergraduates, and a small court called East Court, fashioned out of the little gardens at the back, is a popular suntrap in good weather. Totally uninhabitable and flooded when Emma acquired it, no. 14 was for many years the home of the head chef at the college, Sidney Archer. "My parents moved there in 1925 when I was five. My mother, Grace Archer, ran the house as a lodging house for undergraduates for 52 years," he told me. She died at the age of 95. Were any of those undergraduates destined to be cabinet ministers or bishops? "They mostly all became parsons or farmers," he said. Sid Archer used to play on Parker's Piece as a child and has clear memories of the tradesmen who used to deliver in the street. There was the coalman with his cart, and the milkman who had little cans dangling from the float.

Mrs Agnes Miller, who lives in the basement of 8 Parker Street, which is an Emmanuel College hostel, also lived for many years over the road at no. 15. Those were the days when the houses belonged to Jesus, and her late husband worked as a servant at the college. For 22 years Mrs Miller ran a lodging house there for Jesus College undergraduates. A Londoner, Agnes Miller left school at 13 and went straight into service as a "between" maid doing the stove blackening, the odd jobs and the vegetables for a society family in Upper Grosvenor Street. Later she was in service to the present Lord Derby's grandfather. When she met her husband she was working as a cook for a family who lived near Brighton. Her husband was in service there too, but had to leave "once we were courting". He found work in London. What were their wages in those days? "My husband earned £16 a year, but I didn't get as much. We had all our food and keep, though." Her life in service involved Agnes Miller in a lot of travelling. She went to Scotland on several occasions to cook for the shooting parties. Among her encounters with famous people was a meeting with the Queen Mother, then Duchess of York. "I was in Kent then, and she came down to see the cook in the kitchen and gave her a lovely silver brooch with the royal initials on it."

Lord and Lady Todd came to live at 9 Parker Street in September 1978 when Lord Todd retired. He had been Master of Christ's College for 14 years. The Todds bought their house from Professor Donald McKinnon, the Emeritus Professor of Divinity, who now lives in Aberdeen. Many Cambridge people will know that Lady Alison Todd is president of the Cambridge Committee for Cancer Relief. The committee's present chairman is Lady Stoker, wife of Sir Michael Stoker of Clare Hall. The Stokers have just bought no. 3 Parker Street.

Parker Street is a friendly but noisy street, which is totally unsuited to the volume of heavy traffic which rumbles up and down from Drummer Street and Mill Road and to points north, south, east and west. The Parker Street Residents' Association was founded to tackle the question of the traffic. The founder member of the association was Miss Margaret Pole of no. 7; the present chairman is Lady Todd, and the secretary, Miss Olwen Taylor-Davies, who lives at no. 2. No. 1 Parker Street is well known in Cambridge as the office of the Samaritans, the organisation that guarantees a 24-hours-a-day lifeline to the suicidally unhappy and the depressed. There are always two volunteers on duty, who are known to their clients by their Christian names. People call at the office or ring up; some want to talk and talk for up to three hours at a time. Samaritans are there to listen and help. Their attitude is kind and caring.

8 Park Terrace

22 April 1982

A stranger to Cambridge on a house-hunting mission in the City would be forgiven for lusting after one of those 16 handsome family houses which make up Park Terrace. In an attempt to make the dream come true, he, or more likely she, would rush into the nearest estate agent and say: "Please, is there any chance of one of those Regency houses with that view of Parker's Piece coming on the market?" All hope would be lost, though, when our visitor would have to be told that those are college houses, belonging to Jesus College, and that the families who live there are protected tenants and mostly Fellows of Jesus College. Visions of Jane Austen-style social intrigue in the drawing rooms on the first floor would quickly recede.

There is, of course, as is now common knowledge, talk of sale in the air. Private discussions are going on between Jesus and Emmanuel Colleges, with Emma, not for the first time, wanting to buy Park Terrace from Jesus, for around £1.83 million. While the discussions continue and the planning application goes in, it is interesting to consider the history of these houses, which many of the Cambridge cognoscenti consider to be the finest example of domestic architecture in Cambridge. Professor

The row of 16 houses which make up Park Terrace

Lloyd Austin, a Fellow of Jesus College who lives in one of the flats in Park Lodge, says that "there is nothing in Oxford to compare with it, except perhaps Beaumont Street". "In Park Terrace a controlling ownership, a long-term plan, and sensibility have created an extensive group of town houses, symmetrical in lay-out and mass, of much distinction," says the Royal Commission on Historical Monuments.

Park Terrace is built on the land which used to be known as Nuns' Garden. The Nuns of St Radegund, now Jesus College, built the garden just outside the wall of the Priory of the Dominican Friars, now Emmanuel College. Henry VIII dissolved the Priory in 1538. Emmanuel was founded on the same site less than 50 years later, in 1584, by Sir Walter Mildmay, Chancellor of the Exchequer to Queen Elizabeth I. The clunch wall dividing Emmanuel from the lane at the end of the long gardens of Park Terrace used to be known as the "Town's End"; it goes back to 1238, when the Dominicans first came to Cambridge, and it marked the boundary of their property. The late Professor Ronald Norrish, the distinguished scientist and Nobel prizewinner who was the local expert on Parker's Piece and who lived at 7 Park Terrace, discovered that a small bridge used to go over what became Park Terrace, at one time only a little cart track. The bridge led over a stream which went into the grounds of Emmanuel.

Jesus College says that it is not possible to tell from the charters concerning the Nuns' Field land how it came into the hands of the Priory of St Radegund, except that it must have been at a date before the Dominicans acquired the adjoining land. In a lease of the small close on the north side of the western portion of it dated 1539 this land is described as open field land. In 1577, on the contrary, it is described as a close or pasture, and is said to be parcel of the demesne lands of Jesus College, formerly in the tenure of John Redman, bedell of the University.

Jesus College sold the first building lease on what was to be Park Terrace to a Dr Lee in 1831. In 1835 another lease to a William Mustill was sold for a term of 40 years. The 16 houses overlooking Parker's Piece were built at different times between 1831 and 1840. The terrace consists of five blocks of buildings, says the Royal Commission: "in the middle two houses, nos. 7 and 8, set back behind the building line and designed as a unit; two long terraces of taller houses, nos. 1 to 6 and 9 to 14, on the building line and linked to the first by screen-walls, and, pavilion-like on the extremities, two freestanding houses, Park Lodge and Camden House, complete in themselves." One of the most

attractive features of the two terraces is the cast-iron covered balcony which extends the full length of the first floor of each terrace. The balcony, beautifully restored a year or so ago by Mr Barry Smith of MacKays, has a balustrade and frieze all decorated with an adaptation of the fine Greek honeysuckle motif. The small front gardens, now full of burgeoning spring flowers, were originally fenced by railings on low walls. The railings have been removed.

The first inhabitants of Park Terrace included several clergymen and army officers. By the 1870s the Sturton family had moved in to Park Terrace: Joseph Sturton lived at no. 1, and later his son Richard Sturton was at no. 6. Joseph Sturton, who began with the chemist's shop in Fitzroy Street and became an alderman and mayor, was the astute developer who built Sturton town off Mill Road (see Sturton Street). Mr Robert Potts, who lived at Furness Lodge (now the Telecom manager's office), next to Camden House in Park Terrace, until his death in 1885, was a private University coach, who had been a student at Trinity College in the 1830s. Education records in the County Record Office tell us that Potts was a mathematician of eminence who produced a school edition of Euclid's *Elements*, which sold widely throughout the Empire – from which his well-known interest in Indian students would seem to have arisen. He wanted to establish a hostel for Indian students in Cambridge, in his home in Park Terrace, but "the project was ill-starred because of the opposition of Jesus College to the scheme, opposition which he was unable to overcome". A Miss Robinson was running a ladies' school at no. 10 Park Terrace in 1874. Her next-door neighbour at no. 11 was the Reverend J. Martin, vicar of St Andrew the Great. Later the vicarage must have moved down to the other end of the terrace, because Mrs Edith Brighton, who lived at 2 Park Terrace for many years with her husband Peter, told me from their home at Claremont that 1 Park Terrace in the early 1930s was the vicarage of St Andrew the Great.

By the turn of the century Furness Lodge had become a convent where the sisters of the Institute of Mary lived. Next door in Camden Court were the registered offices of the *Cambridge Graphic*. Park Terrace was at that time largely occupied by dons from a variety of colleges. Henry Robson, the bursar of Sidney Sussex, was living at no. 10. His daughter, Miss J.I.M. Robson, who teaches the viola, is still living in the family home and remembers former inhabitants. She recalls hearing from Miss Frances Scruby, who used to live at Park Lodge, "that Mr Bowes, of the then Macmillan and Bowes, later Bowes and Bowes, built no. 13.

Decorated iron balconies in Park Terrace

George Bowes moved to Newton Road on his marriage to Christine Scruby, and Miss Janet, who kept hens in the back garden in the 1914–18 war (as we did also, and ducks), soon after went to Letchworth. Mrs Rackham, of no. 9, a staunch Labour councillor and alderman, did much for Cambridge. She was a great character, alarming to a schoolgirl, but very kind and a brilliant speaker and an amusing raconteur on warden's duty in the small hours waiting for the 'All Clear'. My mother, too, deserves some mention as one of the first medical students in Glasgow. She did anaesthetics at the Eastern General Hospital and later at Addenbrooke's, and with Dr Haynes started infant welfare clinics.'' Distinguished theologians have lived in Park Terrace. In 1915 Charles Raven, then Dean of Emmanuel and Examining Chaplain to the Bishop of Southwark, and the Reverend F.J. Foakes-Jackson, the famous Dean of Jesus College, were living there. Later, Professor Charles Dodd, the eminent New

Testament scholar, moved in to no. 3. From a later date, Miss Robson adds the names of Denis Nineham, Henry Chadwick and Peter Baelz.

The old coach houses and the pump in the lane at the back of Park Terrace would have been used by the early residents. The coachman's earth closet and the horse's trough were sited at the end of the garden of no. 2. Most of the coach houses have gone – Mrs Brighton remembers the occasion when one of them collapsed. Wartime in Park Terrace was quite eventful. Incendiaries fell on Parker's Piece and in the lane at the back, but miraculously the houses escaped. Mrs Brighton recalls the end of the war. "We knew the war was over when we heard a great shout go up from the troops billeted at Emmanuel College. People rushed and lit a bonfire on Parker's Piece and we all celebrated with our friends. A wonderful moment." Mrs Brighton treasures memories of the days when families used to come and skip on the Piece at Easter time (see Regent Terrace), and when the lamp in the centre was lit by gas.

Professor Austin and his wife, who moved to Flat 2, Park Lodge, after he retired as Drapers Professor of French in 1980, told me that their flat was previously occupied by Frederick Raby, a Fellow of Jesus College who had a fine collection of watercolours and books and worked as a conservationist with the Ministry of Works. Artist Pamela Hughes, who is the ex-president of the Cambridge Drawing Society, has lived with her husband at no. 4 since 1954. Artistic talent thrives in the Terrace. Professor Austin's daughter-in-law Mishtu, who lives at no. 6 Park Terrace, uses the stables at the back of Park Lodge as a studio for her work as a batik artist. Her husband Colin Austin is a Fellow of Trinity Hall and teaches Classics in the University. The Austin family have gone in for a spot of musical chairs at Park Terrace – Colin Austin was in Park Lodge before his father and mother moved in. But Park Terrace is not the sort of street you would want to move from in a hurry, is it?

9 Regent Terrace

10 December 1981

For the cricketing fraternity, a house in Regent Terrace, in the days when Jack Hobbs and Tom Hayward were scoring their centuries on Parker's Piece, must have been the equivalent of a box at Covent Garden. Among the occupants of that motley group of Victorian houses occupying a wedge-shaped piece of land to the south-west side of Parker's Piece was, from 1915 to 1920, none other than Tom Hayward himself. He lived at Alma House, 11 Regent Terrace, now the home of Mrs Helen Richardson, who originally had no idea of the exciting sporting associations attached to her home.

A grand event on Parker's Piece – a feast to celebrate the coronation of Queen Victoria, in 1838. About 15,000 people were entertained, watched by another 17,000

Tom Hayward was one of the most famous Cambridge cricketers of the late 19th century. He lived from 1871 until 1939 and during that time became something of a legend. He played for Surrey with Jack Hobbs, another local celebrity (see Sleaford Street), and visited America and Australia three times. He played in 29 Test matches and his achievements sound like an entry in the Guinness Book of Records. Well into the 20th century his record of 3,518 runs in a season was unbroken. They say that it is for his batting that he will be remembered. He was the first batsman after W. G. Grace to complete 100 centuries. His father Daniel was a well-known player, and so too were his brother and uncle. His father played for Cambridgeshire with Fenner, whose cherry orchard became the University Cricket Ground, even now known as Fenner's.

A special public dinner was held in honour of Tom Hayward in 1902 at which he was presented with a certificate in appreciation of his services to cricket. Eulogistic speeches were made and toasts drunk to the great man. According to a report in the *Cambridge Independent Press*, when Mr Jephson, a prominent member of the Surrey club, responded to the toast, he read a few amusing lines of verse which he had adapted to suit the occasion. This is how the ditty went:

Tom had bought a grand new bat
And some brand new leg guards too;
Scores were easy after that.

Fame at last, see, every brat
Awestruck whispering anew
"Tom has bought a brand new bat."
Did it drive? You'd eat your hat,
If the bowlers looked not blue;
Scores were easy after that.

"Next man in!" The scorers sat
Sharpening bravely, for they knew
Tom had bought a grand new bat.
"Two leg, please" – a gentle pat
Of the block success to woo –
Scores were easy after that.

Down his leg stump crashes flat,
Bitterly poor Tom did rate,
He had bought a grand new bat –
Ducks were bitter after that.

Jack Hobbs described Parker's Piece as probably the finest and most famous public cricket ground in the world. As a boy, Hobbs rose at six and walked for half an hour to practise there before breakfast, and in the summer holidays he played all day and sometimes watched Ranjitsinhji practising at the nets. On this ground Hobbs scored his first century. The story goes that when Ranjitsinhji, the Indian prince, was training the University players, he used to encourage their bowling by putting a sovereign on top of the stumps. The sovereign went to the person who knocked it off! "Without Parker's Piece, Cambridge cricket would long ago have lost its heart. It is the ambition of every six-hitter in the business to hit the clock atop the pavilion which enshrines the name of one of the greatest players of all time, the late Sir Jack Hobbs. He gave Parker's Piece the reputation which is still cherished by sportsmen throughout the world", wrote my colleague David Waterson in the *Cambridge Evening News* in October 1971.

The mixed architecture of Regent Terrace

F. C. Barrett of Girton describes the similarly strong association of the Piece with football: "In 1883 there were eight clubs playing on the Piece, mixtures of Town and Gown players. They were Albert, Camden, Cassandra, Granta, Old Perseans, Printers and Rovers." Early in 1884 an association was formed; the affiliation fee was to be 5 shillings and the county colours cerise and white. A county XI was to be formed to play the University and other counties. Mr Barrett notes that those who attended the first meeting included A. T. P. Dunn, who played for England five times between 1882 and 1887, eventually as captain, and J. P. F. Rawlinson, the England goalkeeper, who became CFA president, a QC and the Cambridge Recorder.

Cricket and football, hockey and rounders and local school sports are among the spectacles which take place on Parker's Piece and which residents of Regent Terrace can watch from their windows. People have ridden on it and skipped on it. Bat and trap was played there until 50 years ago and the annual skipping ceremony on Good Friday was a custom which continued well into the 1930s. Enid Porter described the custom in an article in the *Cambridge Evening News* on 13 April 1963.

"By mid-day the Piece was crowded with family parties, the men of the family, by tradition, turning the ropes while the women skipped, although children made up their own groups too, and jumped up and down over their ropes as they chanted the many well-known skipping rhymes. When the skippers were exhausted they sat down on the grass and ate the food they had brought with them, supplemented by sweets, lemonade and ginger beer bought from the many stalls which, by dinner time, were lining the sides of the Piece. In the afternoon the skipping was resumed, though less energetically than before, and by 3 or 4 o'clock everyone would have had enough of it and the journey home would begin." The skipping rope was usually the family clothes line.

The second world war brought the skipping to an end. By 1948 there were only about three groups of people who continued it, and in that year the stalls had dwindled to one. Miss Porter said that several explanations have been advanced to explain why skipping was performed by adults on Good Friday, the most acceptable being that "the practice was connected with the magical spring-time leaping which was, in ancient times, associated with the growth of crops".

All kinds of celebrations have taken place on Parker's Piece but the most amazing was the Coronation meal of 1838, a lavish tuck-in with a menu which included, among other things, 1,608 plum

Tom Hayward, the cricketer, posed at the wicket in the early 1900s. The picture is autographed "Yours sincerely T. Hayward"

and St Mary's Dole, while Trinity College settled for ground west of the Cam – the Backs, then as now, being the *sine qua non* of a site for prestigious colleges who were or who wanted to be established there.

What did the famous Piece look like in the early days? According to Samuel Page Widnall in his *Gossiping Stroll through the Streets of Cambridge*, the land at first lay in ridges and furrows, with ditches and hawthorn trees around it; on the west side was a small brook ("the new river") on its way to Barnwell Gate and the King's Ditch. It was the resort in spring of the youth of the town, who went there maying. Three college cricket clubs levelled and re-laid part of it to play on, and afterwards it was all levelled and fenced round, thanks chiefly to Charles Humfrey (see Parker Street). Parker's Piece was not always the compact square that we now see. "It was divided by a hedge and ditch starting from somewhere at the back of the Prince Regent Inn, which proceeded in an irregular line towards East Road. The part on the south side of this hedge was called Donkey Common, as well as the land still so named on the other side of the road, a portion of which was enclosed to build a town gaol in 1827–8. This was taken down a few years ago [1879] when Queen Anne's Terrace was built on the site."

How a stream came to Parker's Piece on its way from Hobson's Conduit to Emmanuel and Christ's Colleges is another instalment in the Parker's Piece/ Regent Terrace saga. According to a lecture by the late Professor R. G. W. Norrish of Emmanuel College, who was an authority on the Piece, in about 1616 the Masters of Christ's and Emmanuel conceived the idea of bringing the stream along Hills Road. "So they got the Manciple of Emmanuel College to take over the organisation of bringing the stream along Lensfield Road to the corner where the Catholic Church is now, across the road, where they built a bridge which became known as Sentry Bridge because it was at this bridge that Cromwell was supposed to have posted his sentries when he was occupying Cambridge. After passing the Hadstock or Hills Road, it turned left very soon across Gonville Place and the corner of Parker's Piece. It is still there underground. Before the stream was diverted there, Parker's Piece came up to the main road."

Parker's Piece was cut off from Regent Street by the ditch, and the wedge-shaped area left behind became, say historians, too much of a temptation for the Corporation and also for squatters. The councillors of the time did a bit of wheeling and dealing among themselves and acquired very cheap-

puddings, 1,029 joints of meat, 99 barrels of best ale, and 4,500 loaves of bread. More than half the residents of Cambridge sat down to the feast, the tables being arranged like large spokes radiating from the hub of a wheel.

Parker's Piece is named after a pastrycook who used the land on lease from Trinity College in 1587. It became Corporation property in 1613 when the town and Trinity College did a swap. The town accepted the Piece, made up of St Michael's Dole

ly vacant pieces of land by the roadside – land which was soon to become very valuable. An Inquiry by Royal Commissioners in 1833 to examine the deeds of the discreditable councillors found, for instance, that the land on which the last 10 or 12 shops just south of the University Arms now stand (part of Regent Street and Regent Terrace) was granted to a favoured alderman at a rent of 10 shillings, the purchase money being one guinea! A large portion of the rest of Regent Street on both sides, with a total frontage of 1,386 feet, was, for £24, given to an agent who handed it on to another alderman. As H. P. Stokes wrote in *Outside the Barnwell Gate*, "Anyone who reads the report [of the Royal Commissioners], or who consults the list of Mayors of Cambridge for fifty years previously to the year 1832, will not doubt that the reforms wrought by the Municipal Corporation Act (1835) were called for."

The houses in Regent Terrace are certainly desirable. From the elegant upstairs drawing rooms of Mrs Dorice Ede at 19a Regent Terrace and of Mr and Mrs Michael Linsey at 7 Regent Terrace you look right across the Piece down to Park Terrace and over to Parkside. "It is the biggest front lawn in Cambridge," said Mr Linsey, a musician who is helping his wife Eileen run the Mid-Anglian branch of the British Nursing Association from their home. "We have a good view of the Victorian Fair, of all the cricket matches and of the foreign students who congregate here in the summer. Anything that happens on Parker's Piece or in Regent Terrace is totally transitory. However unpleasant it will go away." Mr Linsey's last remark is a reference to the reputation of Regent Terrace as "Dossers' Alley".

An iron gate used to go across the end of the terrace at Gonville Place, making it into a private road. A lot of traffic uses the road now. As well as local residents several businesses in Regent Street have their back entrance in Regent Terrace: the Prince Regent Inn and DER television rentals, to name two. A lot of people think it is a through road. To deter some of the traffic, residents would like their iron gate back.

The Cambridge and District Branch of the Citizens Advice Bureau have occupied offices at 31 Regent Terrace for six years. They took the premises over from the Royal Navy and Royal Marines Careers Office, now at 92 Regent Street. The CAB office, run by a team of staff augmented by 40 volunteers, answers about 1,600 inquiries a month. "Last year we dealt with 15,500 inquiries, of which 5,737 were personal callers, 9,582 were phone calls and 161 were letters." Above the CAB office is a flat for staff at the University Arms Hotel. Another important establishment in Regent Terrace is the Fairlawn Educational Centre at nos. 12 and 13, where students are prepared for General Certificate of Education O and A level exams. Many years ago 13 Regent Terrace used to be Mrs Cherry's Dance Studio, while in 1915 it was a dancing academy run by the Misses King. No. 7 was the office of the Cambridge General Benefit Society.

A residential and commercial street, Regent Terrace must rank as a street with one of the best views in Cambridge.

10 Mill Road

5 August–2 September 1982

In the Middle Ages, Mill Road was one of the tracks that led out of Cambridge across the Barnwell Fields that ran from Midsummer and Stourbridge Commons to Trumpington Road. Mill Road appears in the old field books as Hinton Way, and at a crossing of tracks on what is now the town side of the railway bridge, there used to be a wayside cross. Until the Enclosure Act of 1806–7 the whole area was nothing but open fields, the only real landmark being the windmill which gave Mill Road its name. The mill stood almost opposite Emery Street on the site of what is now a Chinese restaurant. The beautiful

Bernard and Pauline Wilkinson behind the traditional bacon-slicer at the Meadowsweet Dairy in Mill Road

hand-coloured map of 1830 by R.G. Baker shows the mill and, nearby, a few cottages in the Covent Garden area, but the oldest building actually on Mill Road was the cottage on the nursery in front of St Philip's vicarage. Further down, at the end of Romsey Town, was Polecat Farm, its name going back to medieval times. An earlier map, of 1823, shows the buildings on Polecat Farm with Mill Road petering out into a footpath on marshy ground at Hinton Moor.

We know a little about the mill. A wooden mill described as "near Parker's Piece" was offered on a 40-year lease in an advertisement in the *Cambridge Chronicle* in 1777. It was bought by Charles Humfrey Snr, a timber merchant, who rebuilt it in brick

Christmas lunch in the workhouse in the 1880s

at a cost of £2,000. It stood on that site for another 50 years until the sails were blown off in a gale in 1840. The tower of the mill can be seen in the background of an engraving of a cricket match on Parker's Piece in 1843 which is thought to be the only existing illustration of the Mill Road mill. The site of the mill was offered for sale as arable land in an advertisement in the *Cambridge Chronicle* in 1845.

The important landowners in Mill Road and the surrounding area were Gonville and Caius and Jesus Colleges. Although their land never actually came up to Mill Road, Jesus, who had taken over the Convent of St Radegund, owned everything beyond the original Newmarket–Cambridge railway line. Pre-enclosure records show that they had all the approaches to what later became the railway station. On enclosure, Caius got the tract of land stretching from Gonville Place to Cambridge Place, and on the other side of Mill Road, a great lump of land which included the site of the future Cambridgeshire College of Art and Technology (CCAT). They were the major landowners on Mill Road; the Manor of

Mortimer in Newnham belonged to them, as well as bits and pieces of land listed as Mortimer's Dole in three of the Barnwell Fields, one of them in the Gresham Road area. From the Panton trustees Caius bought two pieces of the large Panton estate (see Abbey Road) which were sold in 1811. The first bit ran down from Mortimer Road nearly to Covent Garden. The second ran down St Barnabas Road and one side of Tenison Road and took in Lyndewode Road. Various swaps were made with Jesus and Corpus Christi Colleges, the other landowners in the Tenison Road area. It was on Caius land in Mill Road that St Barnabas' Church was built; the college donated the site, and the foundation stone was laid in 1869. In the early 19th century the road was developed gradually, as Caius doled it out in large pieces on 40-year building leases.

One of the important 19th-century developments in Mill Road was the building of the workhouse, now the maternity hospital. In fact the oldest surviving building in the road is the administrative block of the maternity hospital, once the frontage of the workhouse. You can see the date 1838 in the brickwork. Why was Mill Road chosen as the site of the workhouse? Leonard Amey, who is an authority

The sign of the Durham Ox

on the history of Mill Road, says that "the authorities as usual dumped it as far out of town as they dared go". The building of the workhouse was the result of the Poor Law Act of 1834 which set up unions of parishes. The parish poor rate was diverted into each union to pay for its workhouse. The original Barnwell Workhouse, in the pre-union days, was further down East Road in what used to be a densely populated area. At the time the new workhouse was built in Mill Road there were quite a few houses going up around the mill site between Covent Garden and that part of Mawson Road which became known as Union Terrace because of the workhouse opposite. Then a few cottages started to go up on the far side of the workhouse. One of these was inhabited by a great English cricketer called Robert Carpenter – one of the first England players and a contemporary of Haywood. A professional cricketer who made a lot of money, Carpenter lived to a ripe old age. On the other side of the road, somewhere between St Barnabas' Church and Tenison Road, there was a substantial

villa, the property of Charles Humfrey, which was sold in 1845 as "the thatched cottage". It later became known as Swiss Cottage. The chaplain to the workhouse lived in it at one time, as did the manager of Headley's Iron Foundry. Swiss Cottage was demolished fairly late in the century.

In 1845 the railway came to Cambridge, but it didn't affect Mill Road very much at that time. "Much more important from the point of view of Mill Road," says Len Amey, "was the removal in 1847 of Headley's Foundry to a site adjoining the railway line, now occupied by the Corporation." One of the Headley partners built himself a substantial house called The Limes between the Foundry and Mill Road. The house is described in the Royal Commission on Historical Monuments as "an early example of the lofty, irregularly-planned house of indeterminate Gothic inspiration that was soon to appear in great numbers in suburban development in most parts of the country". The Limes was later occupied by Sherlock, the railway engineer. By 1850 there were 38 houses listed as rateable in Mill Road, mainly near Covent Garden and the workhouse, together with five railway cottages.

One of the things which hampered development was that Mill Road wasn't very well drained or sewered. The sewer was not laid down until the 1860s; a spur was laid through as far as Covent Garden in 1862 and later extended. Once the sewer was in there was a bit more development, including a successful attempt, in 1865, to hold Caius College to ransom. This is what happened. A block of three acres between Caius holdings and Covent Garden (which had been an orchard or nursery) was acquired by a group of property speculators who put up the land for sale by auction in very small lots. The auction was publicised in the *Cambridge Chronicle*, and Caius had to pay £3,136 to acquire the land and prevent any undesirable development between their holdings.

So by the mid-19th century the Mill Road area had begun to grow. Josiah Chater found "quite a little town in that part of the world" in 1847, although the development of the Romsey Town end of the road did not come until after 1879, and for a long time the whole area remained virtually rural and unknown. In 1870 there were still only 53 houses in the road, compared with 96 in developing Sturton Town and 93 in the Covent Garden area. Let us look now at the Covent Garden side of Mill Road as far as the railway bridge, and note its development between 1866 and 1874, just before the big expansion of the area.In 1866 a stonemason called

Shopping in Mill Road in 1976

R.S. Naylor was living near the Locomotive public house, whose landlord was John Wilson. There were only four other houses listed on that side of the road: J.O. Bradbury lived next to John Wheaton who ran a general shop; his neighbour was B. Reeve, while further down the road lived the Reverend J. Orman. Was he the chaplain at the workhouse?

By 1874 several more people had moved into that side of Mill Road, including a florist called George Tredgett and a music teacher, Edmund John Bilton, who was the senior lay clerk at Trinity College. The road now had numbers and James Watson, a fore-man of engine cleaners at the station, was living at 5 Mill Road next to Daniel Wright, the blacksmith. Another railway worker living in that stretch in 1874 was a ticket collector, Thomas Stone, at no. 12. The street had acquired another pub, the Crystal Palace, at no. 9, and ten years later yet another pub had appeared between Covent Garden and Union Terrace (later Mawson Road), the Windmill, whose landlord, George Bailey, was also a stonemason and sculptor with his own cemetery works.

By 1884 there were quite a few shops on that side of Mill Road, although most of the early shops were just stuck in front of small cottages. There was no purpose-built shopping development until about the late 1880s or 1890s. Among those early shops were two hosiers' and general drapers' – William Warnes

Mr John Howes (centre) with some of the staff at the baker's shop in Romsey Town

at no. 16 and Miss Mary Judd at no. 27. Miss Judd's next-door neighbour was Robert Felton, who had an oil, lamp, colour and paper-hanging warehouse at no. 28. Felton Street must have been named after him, just as Mitcham's Corner in New Chesterton got its name from the draper's on the corner of Victoria Avenue and Chesterton Road. There was a butcher – Thomas Haslop at no. 24 – and a grocer, Frank Ward, at no. 15. John Woods ran the post office at no. 22 and Charles Wallis at no. 21 was a newsagent and stationer who had a toy and music warehouse. Frank Coleman at no. 20 was the baker, pastrycook and confectioner. Further up, beyond Tenison Road and St Barnabas' Church and St Barnabas' Girls' and Infants' School, was the Mill Road Coffee Tavern on the corner of Devonshire Road, next door to Paul Wherle, the watchmaker, jeweller and silversmith. At the other end of the street, just near Covent Garden, lived the Utteridge family, who would have made quite a contribution to community life. Henry Utteridge was a metal turner and his wife, Mrs M.A.R. Utteridge, a dress-maker. They lived at no. 5, three doors away from Charles Utteridge (perhaps father or brother?) at no. 8. George Warland, the cabinet maker, had a furniture warehouse between the Utteridges at nos. 6 and 7.

By 1898 the street had been renumbered and the south side of Mill Road had developed as a busy shopping street serving the railway community. You could buy everything from pianos to tombstones

In the heart of Romsey Town

there! More houses and shops had been built in the part between Mortimer Road and Covent Garden. There were two cycle agents – Seth C. Reeve at no. 2 and Herbert J. Storey, maker of the "Ruby" cycle, at no. 16; and two tailors – G.A. Lofts at no. 8 and B.T. Waits at no. 28. Harry Leavis (father of the critic F.R. Leavis) had his pianoforte warehouse at no. 14, next to the Danish Bacon and Butter Co., now Arjuna Wholefoods, at no. 12. Several of the houses in that particular stretch were given imposing-sounding names. Thus no. 30, the home of draper William Nicholes, was called Commerce House; next door was Taybank House, while no. 34, home of milliner and fancy draper Mrs J.A. Tocock, was Hungerford House (the early residents had certainly travelled!).

At the turn of the century, among the newcomers to the next section of the street, between Covent Garden and Tenison Road, were Eastmans the butchers at no. 54; Freeman, Hardy and Willis, the shoe shop, at no. 62; and Sidney Campkin the chemist at no. 74. The street had also acquired two fishmongers – B.A. Harris at no. 80 and Henry Jenkins at no. 100. By the time of the first world war, Mill Road was clearly established as one of the busiest shopping streets in Cambridge, and some of the shops that were in business in 1913 are still trading there today. W.T. Naylor, the popular fruiterer and greengrocer at no. 94, is one of the oldest businesses in the street, as is the Meadowsweet Dairy Company at no. 68, which has been run by the Wilkinson family since 1916. "My father-in-law Alfred Wilkinson came here as manager in 1916

from Yorkshire," said Mrs Pauline Wilkinson, whose husband Bernard was born at the shop. The company then belonged to Goodwin Foster Brown Ltd, who had wholesale grocery businesses in Oxford, Yarmouth and Dudley as well as Cambridge. When they sold off the shops Alfred Wilkinson bought the Cambridge branch, in 1930. The Meadowsweet Dairy Co. Ltd is one of those endearingly old-fashioned grocers, with an old bacon machine and a clock which dates back to 1948 and proclaims the attractions of Craven A. When Mrs Wilkinson first came to work in the shop they used to "weigh everything up", and during the second world war they served out the rations.

In 1912 the Playhouse was opened at the junction of Mill Road and Covent Garden. It was mostly demolished in the early 1960s and is now the Fine Fare supermarket. For many years no. 110 Mill Road was a shop belonging to Smart and Son, the clothiers, tailors and outfitters who also had a shop at 11 Market Street. Later the shop became a hairdresser's, but it is now Cam Audio, specialists in hi-fi equipment. Herbert Robinson had a radio, television, bicycle and domestic appliance business for many years at 2 Mill Road. Stefan Fabish from Poland came to 62 Mill Road in the 1950s. One of Cambridge's most popular butchers, he is currently president of the Cambridge and District Master Butchers' Association. This side of Mill Road still has a good range of shops, but there is a more bohemian atmosphere about the street than there was, say, ten years ago.

Now let's turn to the north side of the road. Petersfield and Donkey Common – the two bits of "green belt" marking the approach to Mill Road at the City end – were added to the map at the time of the Enclosure Act in 1806–7 to make up the number of common grazing spots in the City. Donkey Common has been more or less absorbed by the Parkside swimming pool – before that there were Nissen huts on it – but Petersfield is still undeveloped. It is a reasonably pleasant urban park with a few swings and a slide, a breath of air a stone's throw from the traffic.

In the early part of the 19th century, when Mill Road was still a track across fields, what later became Mill Road Cemetery used to be a cricket ground. But the first building to go up on the north side of Mill Road was the workhouse (see above), in 1838. By 1866 a few houses and two pubs – the Swan and the Durham Ox – had been built near the workhouse, together with Headley's Iron Foundry, which had found a new home in Mill Road in 1847 following a disastrous fire in 1846 in the old premises on Market Hill. The Mill Road site adjoined the new railway line – a really strategic position. As already mentioned, one of the partners, I.J. Headley, built himself a substantial house called The Limes. Gwydir House nearby was sold "by direction of the mortgager" in 1862, and in the early 1870s W.I. Basham built Petersfield Lodge at the other end of Mill Road (now the postal sorting office).

It was in the late 1870s that Corpus Christi College started to develop its land on the workhouse side of the road, with Emery Street having the edge on Perowne Street, selling plots for rather superior house building. Alderman Samuel Leggett Young, JP and mayor of Cambridge 1892–3, was living in Petersfield Lodge by 1884. The adjoining ground was occupied by John Swan and Son, the upholsterers. In the next stretch, before the entrance to the cemetery, Robert W. Feaks, the seedsman, fruiterer and florist, ran the Covent nursery. In Pulling Terrace, between the cemetery and Emery Street, there lived in 1884 an earthenware merchant, an Inland Revenue officer, a railway ticket collector and a coal agent. In the next section, between Emery Street and Perowne Street, lived a similar sprinkling of commercial people, including a coal agent, a commercial traveller and a travelling draper. A factory surgeon for the Cambridge district called F. Russell Hall lived at 10 Pulling Terrace. Just before the site of the Cambridge Union Workhouse, to give it its proper title, were two villas, Emery Villa, occupied and possibly built by John Russell Denson, the builder and contractor, and Percy Villa, home of John O'Currey. (Why Percy? Any link with the Duke of Northumberland?)

Luke Hosegood and his wife were master and matron of the workhouse in the 1880s, having taken over from Mr and Mrs W. Bounds. The Hosegoods feature in the detailed photographs of the workhouse in the 1880s which belong to the Cambridge and County Folk Museum. Beyond the workhouse came the Durham Ox pub, landlord Thomas Twinn. Mrs Naomi Slater ran the tobacconist's next door at no. 48. Sturton Town Hall, built in 1881, was the Working Men's Liberal Club and Reading Rooms for many years. The hallkeeper lived next door. The hall was named after Joseph Sturton, who bought 28 acres in Mill Road when the estate of the Reverend J. Geldart was sold in 1879. The Town Hall has also been a Salvation Army hall and a variety hall, and more recently it functioned as a cinema, the Kinema, which opened in 1917 and closed in the early 1970s. Robert Carpenter, the professional cricketer, used to lived at no. 45, just by Sturton Town Hall. In 1884 the surgeons Turnell and Rygate had consulting rooms at the corner of Gwydir Street and Mill Road, next to the corn merchant called Richard Tofts. The Union Workhouse Vegetable Gardens were further down in Kingston Terrace by Gothic House, the home of Algernon Lyon, a solicitor who was also captain of the Cambridge Volunteer Fire Brigade. Then came James Headley's house The Limes, adjoining his Eagle Foundry and Coprolite Mills. There was only a crossing and foot passengers' bridge over the Great Eastern Railway in 1884. The bridge wasn't built until 1889, but the railway cottages were there, the homes of railway inspectors, platelayers and a guard. The original wooden footbridge is now over the line that crosses Coldham's Common.

Nearly 15 years later we find the Mill Road Library established on the north side. It was called then the Cambridge Free Library and Reading Room (Barnwell Branch). Philanthropy had arrived in Mill Road by then, because next door to the library at no. 117 was the Liverpool Victoria Legal Friendly and Medical Aid Society's branch office, with a resident agent called Charles Motthers. There was a building society too – the Cambridge Peers' Economic Building Society, at no. 73. The north side of Mill Road was popular with doctors, surgeons and dentists at the turn of the century. Stanley Wood, the physician and surgeon, lived at Gwydir House. Further down, Palm Villa on the corner of Guest Road was the home of Upendra K. Dutt, another surgeon. Dentist A.S. Rayner of Clifton House, no. 97, would make your "artificial teeth" for you and James Waterton ran the Artificial Teeth Depot at Cobden House, no. 51.

It was still the era of the horse and cart. In 1913 Herbert Guyver was a harness maker and saddler living near the White Swan at no. 107, not far from

W.L. Norman, the horsekeeper at Cornetta Villa, no. 101. An intriguing resident of Mill Road then was Councillor Newton Digby, who was described in the street directory as the University and Sandringham Intelligence Service. He lived at Mill House, no. 9. This was clearly one of the more substantial residences in Mill Road; likewise the suburban-sounding Palm Villas, Laurel Villa, Esbourn House, Gainsboro House and Alexandra House, nos. 19–25.

The County Council had intended to turn the old workhouse into a maternity hospital for many years before the outbreak of the second world war, but then the scheme had to be postponed because during the war the buildings were acquired for an emergency hospital for troops and patients evacuated from London hospitals. At the end of the war part of the hospital was converted into maternity wards. By 1946 the conversion was complete and the hospital was accepted as a Part I Midwifery Training School. It has been the excellent Mill Road Maternity Hospital ever since, but the end of an era is coming. The maternity hospital will soon move into new buildings at Addenbrooke's, where it will be renamed the Rosie.

Romsey Town from Mill Road bridge; a postcard of 1910

The big development of Romsey Town took place after the 1880s, but long before that there were one or two little buildings dotted about in the fields. Take Romsey Cottage, later to become Romsey House. The cottage was built about 1840. In 1846 it was owned by a plumber of St Andrew's Street, called Edward Favell. He paid rates of £8 a year on the house, and £30 a year on the land – acres of garden and pasture. Then in 1851 the Cambridge–Newmarket railway line was opened. It cut right through the grounds of Romsey Cottage. Favell was given a private level crossing and compensation which enabled him to buy land on the other side of Mill Road, on the site of Hemingford Road. After Favell's death his farm was sold to George Johnson, a surgeon of St Andrew's Street. Johnson had acquired 17½ acres from Favell's estate, which was rated in 1858 at £15 for the house and buildings and £80 for the land. Johnson bought further land on both sides of the railway from the Serocold Estate. The Serocolds were a Cherry Hinton family. After Johnson's death in 1865 the property was held in trust for his wife and son. It was let to a man called Remington Pratt of Cherry Hinton, who farmed just under 60 acres of it. Part of the land was sold for building in 1880. The house was then rebuilt and incorporated in a larger Romsey House; the solicitor James Prior lived there until the turn of the century.

Mill Road, Cambridge.

The Mill Road Baptist Chapel Sunday School in the early 1900s

It is the only one of the biggish suburban houses still remaining, although the grounds are smaller than they were originally. Romsey Road, by the side of Romsey House, led down to Polecat Farm and Romsey Terrace.

The nursery and market garden on the site of St Philip's vicarage lasted very nearly 100 years. It was at one time run by Josiah Chater's brother, and when he died his widow carried on the business. A later owner was a market gardener called Alfred Dawson. In 1898 the nursery, which ran from no. 242 to no. 256 Mill Road, was called the Beaconsfield Nurseries. Even in 1884 the Romsey Town end of Mill Road was only sparsely developed. On the south side, starting from the Cherry Hinton Fields, there was only the Royal Standard and Romsey House before the nursery and market garden, although Hobart, Marmion, Madras and Malta Roads were already there. There were only three houses between the nursery and Hope Street, although plots for building four or five houses had been earmarked. An architect and builder called William Saint was living in Iva House. He probably did much of the local building work. An engine driver and two railway clerks were living between Hope Street and Cockburn Street, and there was one shop, belonging to a confectioner and general dealer, Mrs Elizabeth Bowden. Her husband Mark Bowden was another builder. There were a few key shops between Cockburn Street and Argyle Street: a bootmaker, a greengrocer, a butcher and a grocer and general dealer. The houses and shops, with a few exceptions like the houses in Measham Terrace

further up, were not numbered. One of the important residents of Measham Terrace must have been the G.E.R. district inspector, H. Watson, who lived at no. 1 next to the G.E.R. grounds.

By the turn of the century, Mill Road in Romsey Town was more or less complete. Within 15 years a community whose raison d'être was to serve the railway had grown up in a self-contained Victorian township. Railway platelayers lived next to the railway engine drivers. Their neighbours were railway guards, clerks and firemen. The railway workers and their families would have relied on the large number of small shops and businesses which developed in the area. There were three or four bakers and pastrycooks on the south side at the turn of the century, and several butchers, tobacconists, grocers and greengrocers. Romsey Town Post and Money Order Office and Savings Bank was established early on in the development of Romsey Town, and so was the Mill Road Baptist Chapel, founded in 1881, and the Salisbury Working Men's Conservative Club. The premises of the Romsey Labour Club in Mill Road were built later, between 1925 and 1928. The post office started further up the road, towards the bridge at no. 230. It moved later to its present site at no. 240. The Rayner family have run the post office since Maurice Rayner's father Reginald took it over in about 1920.

Maurice Rayner, who has lived in Romsey all his life, has clear memories of rural Romsey. "I can remember how they used to drive the cows from Curtis' Dairy in Hope Street down Catherine Street to the common." He remembers the old women with their poke bonnets and the funeral hearses with the plumes on top. Then there was the muffin man and the man with the performing monkey. The railwaymen often named their houses after other towns such as Gloucester and Croydon. Perhaps they had been there on train journeys. But there was the odd joke name like Engiadina Cottage. That was no. 166, the home in 1913 of a coachsmith called Alfred Wild.

Miss W.M. Francis of Madras Road remembers Romsey's medical practitioners. "Dr Burns lived in the house next to Mill Road Library in the early years of the century before the motor car was in general use. Dr Burns walked everywhere. He was quite a little man, and would come any time if called, and always seemed to have time for his patients. He ran a club and for twopence a week one had medical advice and medicine. If it was a home visit, the medicine had to be fetched from the surgery at his house. If it was a surgery visit, the medicine was mixed while one waited. This surgery was also the dispensary, so one sat in there with the walls covered with shelves of bottles and jars. I can see him now holding up a cone-shaped measure, putting in this and that, pouring it into a bottle, filling it up with water, shaking it, writing a label and sticking it on. The label always had 'shake the bottle' printed on it. On the opposite side of Mill Road, at the corner of St Barnabas Road where the bank is now, was a chemist called Flanders. He failed to get his

qualifications as a doctor but many people went to him with common complaints and were quite satisfied. He would also extract teeth, but as he did not use any pain killers, he did not get many customers."

One hundred years ago the north side of Mill Road in Romsey Town, like the south side, was sparsely populated. Most of the houses were modest Victorian dwellings, but there were one or two key residences and buildings. The big house was Mill Villa, afterwards The Lodge, which stood on the site of the Broadway. It was offered for letting in 1867, and for many years, at least from 1884 until the first world war, it was the home of Councillor George Smith, who was a JP and Bailiff of the Borough. A Miss Smith lived on there into the 1930s. The Lodge was demolished and the site developed in the late 1930s, when 14 shops were built with flats above, stretching from Cavendish Road to Sedgwick Street. In 1884, the other houses were modest terrace dwellings, the homes of several carpenters and railwaymen, who lived in Geldart Terrace, or further down beyond Ross Street, then called Butt Row, in Oak Terrace or Ivy Villas. A site had been chosen for the Hospital for Infectious Diseases (Brookfields Hospital), but it hadn't yet been built. Beyond the site of the hospital stretched the Cherry Hinton Fields. It was all open countryside then.

St Philip's Church was also established in Mill Road by the early 1890s. The church had started off

Romsey House, Mill Road

in a rented cottage in Butt Row in 1878. Later in that year a wooden church, seating nearly 100 worshippers, was built at the junction of Ross Street and St Philip's Road and was called St Philip's. In 1882 the wooden building was moved to the corner of Thoday Street and Mill Road, its present site. The foundation stone of the present church was laid in 1889 by Professor C.C. Babington and was dedicated by Lord Alwyn Compton, the then Bishop of Ely, on 1 May 1890. Two years later it was consecrated, and the following year the parish of St Philip's was formed. The substantial vicarage was built opposite, on the site of the nursery described above. A former vicar of St Philip's, the late A.G. Hunt, who was inducted on 21 October 1928 and who died in January 1962 at the age of 80, was one of the oldest active parish priests in the Ely Diocese. He is remembered with affection by many of the people who have lived their lives in Romsey Town.

By the turn of the century most of the development of the north side of Mill Road in Romsey Town was complete in its original form. German Cottages and Brookfield Cottages had been built down by the level crossing over the G.E.R. line. There was a Brook Villa, a Brookfield House and Brookfield Nurseries all near the road leading to the fields near the Sanatorium, as Brookfields Hospital was then called. Next to the Sanatorium was the Romsey Town Cement and Lime Company; the proprietors were Thoday and Co. Thoday was the big local builder, who is said to have named Catherine Street after his wife. John Daisley ran the Mill Road Dairy at 229 Mill Road, but there weren't many shops on the north side in Romsey Town in the early days, so Peak's at 261 Mill Road must have been a popular shop. William Peak was a general agent for Sutton and Co.'s parcel dispatch, while Mrs E. Peak ran a grocer's shop. At 299 Mill Road, just beyond Hemingford Road, was William Lyon, the chemist. Up at 193 Mill Road, nearly at the junction with Thoday Street, was George Reynolds, who dealt in milk, butter, eggs and confectionery. His next-door neighbour at no. 191 was a bootmaker and furniture dealer called William Barrand. One of the most patronised shops was the Co-op at

nos. 177–179, which was going strong in the 1890s. The metamorphosis into the revamped supermarket on the same site came many years later. In the early days the Co-op stood next to Jarman and Co., the brewers and beer retailers at 175 Mill Road, and George French, the corn and seed merchant (see Catherine Street).

Frank Ward ran a popular grocer's and baker's at Cavendish House, at the junction of Mill Road with Cavendish Road. Between Beaconsfield Terrace and Great Eastern Street there were two more shops: a bootmaker, J. Childerhouse, at 143 Mill Road, and a greengrocer, confectioner and newsagent, J. Rumbelow, at 139 Mill Road. You can imagine all the railwaymen popping in to Rumbelow's for their purchases on their way to and from the station. Between Great Eastern Street and the bridge built in 1889 the houses were occupied by railway inspectors, clerks and signalmen who were able to live almost over the shop, as it were. Turpin's timber yard was a well-known spot in Mill Road for many years. The street directory for 1913 lists John Turpin, a "measure maker", at 307 Mill Road, but by 1925 he is listed as a timber merchant at 313 Mill Road. What happened was that when their bushel and peck measures were no longer required, John Turpin and his sons turned to cricket bats. Later they began to supply woods for local builders and one of them, John L. Turpin, set up in the timber trade. The local boys used to go to Turpin's timber yard to collect sawdust for their pet rabbits. Almost next to Turpin's yard, A. Macintosh and Sons ran the Cambridge Iron Foundry for many years. They sold the site to Frank Holland, the proprietor of Dutch's Corner Garage in the early 1960s. Dutch's Corner is one of the landmarks of Romsey Town (for more about it, see Ross Street).

Not many changes have taken place in Romsey Town since its evolution as a residential area 100 years ago. It has remained untouched by a lot of modern developments, and although the shops have changed over the years, there are still a few of the old families and shopkeepers left like the Raynors, and Howes, the bakers, and John Palmer, the chemist. It is a friendly, busy part of the road.

11 Suez Road

20 May 1982

Suez Road, with its distinctively old and new sections, is one of those streets in Romsey Town where the residents romance about steam engines, and remember the cry of the call-boy telling the railway workers what time they had to be on duty at the station.

Since the turn of the century Suez Road, which like most streets off Mill Road was fashioned out of the Barnwell Fields, has been home to legions of L.N.E.R. drivers, guards, boiler-makers, firemen and fitters, who made their way to work up the side of the old G.E.R. line – the old Great Chesterford–Newmarket branch line that ran down what later became Marmora Road. Gardeners there regularly turn up relics of that line, like rusty old iron and nails. The line was used for the storing and cleaning of carriages. Mrs Muriel Reynolds, who moved to Suez Road from London in 1913 as a girl of 13, used to hop on the pilot engine to get an unofficial lift up to the station, where she worked as a telegraphist. At the Cambridge telegraph office in 1918 she took the message that hostilities had ceased in the first world war. Going in the other direction, the line terminated at the Norman Cement Works near a small signal box known as the Brookfields Box, under the jurisdiction of the Fulbourn station master. Every day empty wagons were taken to the sidings at the works to be filled. Norman Cottages, in old Suez Road, were built in 1907 for the cement workers.

When the cartographers were compiling the Ordnance Survey map in 1886, there were no houses in Suez Road, just an orchard and a timber yard. But by 1891, a cutler and scissor grinder called Philip Walton and a corn dealer by the name of Arthur Odell were living on the east side of the street just off Mill Road. The G.E.R. line ran along the bottom of the old Suez Road behind a hedge. Edward Tebbit, a butcher, and a man called John Palmer were established there in 1898. During the next three years building began on the west side, and cottages there were inhabited by a Mrs Leader, by a poulterer called C. Tighe, and by their neighbours, Ellis Creek, a labourer, and H.J. Pauley.

Street numbering began in 1904, the year that

Arthur Forsdyke, the carpenter, moved in to no. 5, where his large family of six sons and two daughters was born. His son Herbert (Bert) Forsdyke of Ross Street, a well-known and much respected Romsey railwayman, vividly remembers his childhood in Suez Road. "Suez Road and neighbouring Malta and Cyprus Roads were connected by a labyrinthine network of passages and pathways in which the children used to play." The Forsdykes' neighbours in Suez Road were nearly all railwaymen. "A copper named Kidd lived at no. 1, driver Wenham at no. 3, driver Maskell at no. 7, guard Tabbitt at no. 9 and old Mr Dowdy, the painter, at no. 11. Then we had the Jakes, Woollards, Bendalls and Howards – they all had a lot of children."

The old birdcatcher of Madras Road fascinated the young Bert Forsdyke and his friends. "On summer days you could see him with a large cage and nets on his back going to Coldham's Common. He pegged out his call birds between two large nets and placed some bird seed on the ground. When the birds came down to feed he pulled the nets over them. He kept the bullfinches, chaffinches, goldfinches, greenfinches, linnets and sparrows and let the others go. He sold the finches and linnets at twopence each and the sparrows at twopence a dozen. Mum often bought a dozen and made a 'spijic' pie with the sparrows and shin of beef seasoned with onions and mixed herbs. Lovely grub." Many Romsey boys had trap cages in those days. "They put a call bird in the bottom of the cage. On the top was a trap door which was left open with a seed tray balanced on it. The call bird whistled and when a bird came down to feed on the tray the door closed and trapped the bird."

Henry Taylor, the railway policeman, moved into 1 Norman Cottages in 1913 with his family. They had come from London. His daughter, Mrs Muriel Reynolds, had been living at 30 Suez Road since it was built. "My parents moved in and rented no. 22, now no. 30, in 1915. Their landlord was Robert Crown, the builder in Mill Road. My husband Dick bought the house from Mr Crown in 1926, the year of the General Strike." For 50 years Richard (Dick) Reynolds worked for the railway emergency service

The Rev. Peter Phenna and his wife, Pam, inside St Martin's Church

– "he went out with the accident van". Sometimes he was called to work at 4 a.m., but 6 a.m. was the time when he was expected to report for duty. Where, I asked Mrs Reynolds, did the children play? "Oh, at the Planny." The "Planny" was a plantation by the level crossing called Marriott's Crossing on Malta Road. "The railway used to put on flower shows there and it was safe to play. When my first son was born, I used to put the sewing machine on the pram and do my work at the Planny."

Three borough policemen lived in Suez Road in the early days. They were Mr Kidd, Mr Kirk, and PC Frederick Cornwell, whose home was 36 Suez Road, formerly 3 Norman Cottages. Today no. 36 is the home of John Mayhew, who teaches nurses at Fulbourn Hospital and is doing a PhD on anorexia nervosa. He is also the representative for the whole of Romsey on the General Improvement Area (G.I.A.) committee. The current preoccupation of those who live in Suez Road is through traffic.

Mr William Bacon and his wife keep the only shop, a grocer's at no. 49 Suez Road. It was a general stores in 1932–3 run by W. Tilley, and W.M. Gray and A.B. Ladds had it in 1955. Ten years later it was called the Suez Road Stores. There was a fish and chip shop at no. 45a for many years – in 1955

A parade of Girl Guides in Suez Road in 1953

Jock's fried fish dealers, in 1965 the Modern Fisheries. Later no. 45a became Cambridge Precision Ltd, a firm which makes contact lenses. They have recently moved to new premises in Gwydir Street. No. 45a was once a blacksmith's. On the opposite side of the street, back in the 1930s and possibly earlier, Stanley Quinney, a pastrycook who lived at 42 Suez Road, ran a general patisserie next door at no. 40.

One of the first people to move in to the council houses built in 1927 on land belonging to Jesus College, in what they call new Suez Road, was Mrs Elsie Mabel Allsop, who is 81. "I've been here since February 1927," said Mrs Allsop, whose husband Arthur died earlier this year. The Allsops, both Derbyshire born and bred, moved to Suez Road from the temporary accommodation that had been their home for four years in Burrell's Walk, on the site of the Great Eastern Hospital built there during the first world war. "When we first came to Suez Road we were all young people here." The late Arthur Allsop, who used to sell his fine tomatoes to the staff of the Sedley Day Nursery, beyond his garden, was a musician who worked at the Central Cinema playing the double bass for the silent pictures for eight years until, as his widow put it, "the talking pictures put him out of work". He went to the Tivoli on Chesterton Road and the Rendez-Vous in Magrath Avenue for a while after that. As a musician he had been earning £4 a week. He then looked for work at St John's College, who offered him 35 shillings and "as much beer as you like".

That wasn't a wage on which to support the family, so eventually he got a job as a postman and worked for the Post Office for 30 years until he retired. After his official retirement, he had a small job in Joshua Taylor's despatch department, and later in the Leys School Tuck Shop. Like Mrs Allsop, her neighbour across the street, Mr H.W. Beamis, another of the original residents of new Suez Road, works hard at his garden. He remembers the four poplar trees which used to stand sentinel at the corner of Hobart Road, and the crab-apple trees which were a popular feature of most gardens. Mr Beamis, a builder who during the second world war built Prisoner of War camps in Cambridge, deplores the decline in garden standards in his part of Suez Road.

For the past 40 years, the Sedley Day Nursery, which opened on 12 June 1942, has provided a lifeline to many Cambridge children and their families. Built as a war-time measure for the children whose mothers were working in local factories for the war effort, it is open for 50 weeks of the year from 8.30 a.m. until 5 p.m. and has about 45 children from six weeks old to school age. In the early days it opened at 8 a.m. and the children were given breakfast. When Mrs Jean Watson, the matron, first went to the Day Nursery in 1947, parents paid 5 shillings a week. The cost went down to 9*d* a day and then went up to 3*s* 9*d*. The charge is now 44*p* a day to cover the cost of tasty-looking lunches. The nursery is a safe spot, tucked away off Suez Road at the back of the Sedley school. The children were playing happily in the sunshine riding little trikes and singing "Old Macdonald had a farm", which had an appropriate ring for a bright summer's day, on the morning that I called.

The first step towards the establishment of what is now the thriving church of St Martin's in Suez Road – between 250 and 300 people worship there on a Sunday morning – came in 1932, when St Paul's decided to build the Suez Road Mission Hall for members of the congregation living in the area. The hall was erected, according to the plaque, "through the gracious gift of Mrs E.M. Rowcroft on a site generously given by the Master and Fellows of Jesus College for the furtherance of God's work in the parish of St Paul's Cambridge". The Mission Hall was set in the midst of fields and allotments and it was several years before a road was built. "It was a muddy track called the Bumps," said Mrs Olive Moore of Hobart Road. In 1961 St Martin's – which has just celebrated its golden jubilee – became an independent parish and the new church was built. Peter Barrett was the first vicar. His successor in 1969 was Peter Phenna, who reminded me that the year was "the one in which Apollo 11 landed on the moon". Today St Martin's is the focal point of the local community, providing a full-time day care centre, an Over 60's Club, a Women's Fellowship and a very strong youth movement called the Campaigners. They have opened a new church hall over in Ancaster Way, in the same way as St Paul's opened the original Mission Hall in Suez Road. A family hostel for the mentally handicapped and a hostel for the physically handicapped which is being built by the Granta Housing Association on a site opposite the church are among the community projects that this wonderfully active church is supporting.

12 Ross Street

4 June 1981

Prospective taxi drivers are expected to know that Ross Street, off Mill Road, is the longest street in Cambridge. As Mr Papworth of 213 Ross Street said to me the other morning: "Once you get walking down this street you know you have got somewhere to walk." And where you walk to is down Ross Street to Coldham's Lane and Coldham's Common, where the rifle butts used to be. It was after those rifle butts that Ross Street got its original names: Volunteer Butts Row, then Rifle Butt Row and later Rifle Butt Road. The name Ross carries on the shooting connection – he was the champion shot of England in 1861. The Cambridge Rifle Club, the first in the country, was established in May 1859. Later in the same year the 8th Cambridgeshire Rifle Volunteers were established, the members – townspeople and members of the Working Men's College – wearing light grey. The corps was maintained from the funds of the Rifle Club and used a shooting range on Mill Road. The approach to the range would have been down Rifle Butt Row. When the Prince of Wales opened the new University Rifle Ground in Grange Road, Ross, the champion of England, fired five shots at 800 yards, which constituted the opening of the ground. Good old Ross. He must have been a crack shot for many years, because Rifle Butt Road didn't become Ross Street until the late 1880s. By 1891 it is Ross Street in the street directory.

First, though, back to 1811 for a moment, and a look at the enclosure map of that year. Mill Road is shown as a private road which petered out into a footpath about where Tenison Road is today. Our Rifle Butt Row was part of the Panton estate (see Abbey Road). By 1878 building was under way in Rifle Butt Row – some of the earliest development in Romsey Town. There was Butt Terrace a little way down on the east side, and two carpenters, a clerk and a printer lived there. Then came Butt Row, a row of 12 houses which were the homes of several railway workers. An engine driver, a railway servant, a fireman, a platelayer, and a guard were among the early inhabitants of Butt Row. Mrs Elizabeth Bell, "Granny" Bell to Ross Street folk, lives at 59 Ross Street behind the shop which used to belong to her husband William Bell, the butcher. She remembers that "you used to be able to stand in the street by Butt Row and look down and see the rifle butts on the Common". Granny Bell is 91.

You can see Butt Row and Butt Terrace on the Ordnance Survey map of 1886. The map also shows Danesbury House, a large house set in its own grounds which stood at the corner of Ross Street and Mill Road on the east side, where Dutch's Corner is today. Mr Bert Forsdyke, of 157 Ross Street, remembers that the house was taken over by an undertaker by the name of Newman. The house was then demolished and the site was bought by a Mr Holland, who built premises for a yeast store. Later his son added a frontage for the sale of cars and the supply of petrol. (The name Dutch's Corner is an obvious local pun on the name of Holland.) Today the site is occupied by Woodwards, a firm which supplies typewriters and accounting machines. Locals remember Danesbury House as "a lovely red brick house".

In 1895 what was to become St Philip's Boys' School in Ross Street is listed in the street directory as St Barnabas' Boys' School. By 1901 it is called St Philip's Boys' School, which must have been the year when the two churches separated into independent parishes. By 1906 the two parishes had nearly 10,000 inhabitants between them, according to Eglantyne Jebb's *Cambridge: A Brief Study in Social Questions*. George Flavell, listed in the street directory as headmaster of the school, must have moved a few years later to be headmaster of Romsey School. Bert Forsdyke, a former pupil of Romsey School, who went on to have a distinguished career with the G.E.R., remembers George Flavell as his headmaster. St Philip's is now a mixed infants' school. Since the last war it has been considerably altered and greatly improved. In the first world war, the playing fields used to be the boys' allotments; during the second world war underground air-raid shelters were constructed beneath them.

Like St Philip's School, most of the original houses in Ross Street belong to the 1890s. On the west side we start at the Mill Road end with Osbourne House, which Mrs Amy Francis, of 51 Birdwood Road, who lived as a child at 133 Ross Street, believes was built for the curate of St Philip's. The houses on that side numbered 3 to 55 are all constructed to the same design; several have names as well as street numbers. Further down past the school are 18 houses which were built in 1912 by John Brignell, the builder. Until the 1930s Ross Street terminated at the Brignell terrace. Then it was developed across what had originally been fields and later allotments. The Ross Street council houses

were built in 1934, when the street was joined up to Coldham's Lane.

Alderman Ernest Gill, who was mayor of Cambridge in 1967–8, remembers rural Ross Street. He was born in 1895, and recalls the smallholding belonging to a Mr Bainbridge that lay in the heart of the agricultural land on the east side of Ross Street. "I used to see him taking his cows across the big meadow to Vinery Road and into Seymour Street." Romsey residents remember the recreation ground, which lies between Ross Street and Vinery Road, being constructed from allotment land in 1922. Mrs Amy Francis (née Scarff), whose father was an engine driver, saw the "rec" being made. "It was all

Mr Bert Forsdyke, president of the Romsey Bowls Club, poised for action

Pupils at St Philip's Junior School

long grass then, and my friend and I used to make secret houses by winding round the grass and then flattening it down in the middle. No one could see us. All the paths for the 'rec' were made up of clinker and old bits of china. We used to go round and see what pretty bits of china we could find." Before the second world war, the "rec" was used annually for the Romsey Town Flower Show and for sports meetings. Top cyclists and athletes used to compete there.

You can't talk about the "rec" without mentioning the Romsey Bowls Club. Its president, Bert Forsdyke, gives a glowing progress report. "The Bowls Club has been very successful over the years, and has provided many representatives for the County matches, County League and District League matches. A number of the players have won major County honours" – not least Mr Forsdyke himself, who is also president of the British Railways Staff Association Club. Another stalwart is Cyril Atkin, who has been secretary of the Bowls Club for many years and is also secretary of the County Bowls League. His late father John Atkin, also of Ross Street, likewise served the club for a number of years.

Next to the "rec" on the east side are flats which used to be a children's home. Mrs Francis remem-

bers that a row of cottages formerly stood there, and she saw the children's home being built. "On Saturday afternoons we used to love to play there while they were building it. In those days children didn't do any vandalising." The children's home in Ross Street was for the illegitimate children of the girls from the old workhouse in Mill Road. Mrs Annie Amey was in charge of the nursery at the workhouse, now the Mill Road Maternity Hospital: "I looked after the babies until they were three, then they went to the children's home in Ross Street. I used to take the mothers along from the workhouse on a Saturday afternoon to visit their children. The mothers wore dresses made of pillow ticking, so did their little children, whom I used to take out as babies on Mill Road. I couldn't bear to see the children dressed like that, so I collected things from people, and with the aid of my sewing machine made the children little dresses."

Just up from the children's home at 128 Ross Street is a house which used to be the Ross Stores, at one time a thriving general stores. Mrs Francis knew the shop when it first opened after the first world war. "Mrs Holmes opened up her front room there as a sweet and general shop after her husband lost his job. There was a lot of unemployment then, and two other women in the street did the same." Younger residents remember the Ross Stores as "Tedders". Mrs Doreen Kavanagh, who was born

Mr William Bell (in apron) outside his butcher's shop, before 1914. With him are his sister and his delivery boy Gilbert Barber

at 186 Ross Street in 1940 (and now lives at no. 228) speaks warmly of Mrs Tedders, "who sold everything". Mrs Kavanagh also remembers the street party in Ross Street held after the end of the second world war to welcome home the soldiers. To a little girl it must have been a rare treat. Mothers laid on the food, and the children wore fancy dress.

Back to the shops now, and back up the street to 59 Ross Street, which for many years was W. Bell, family butcher. "Granny" Bell told me about it: "For 50 years my husband kept the shop, which used to be a little grocer's when my husband first bought it. I think he was one of the first butchers in Cambridge to have a refrigerator, for a lot of the butchers in the town came to look at it. My husband was vice-president of the Master Butchers' Association." His father was a coachman to the Duke of Bedford. Before she married, Mrs Bell (née Archer) lived at 122 Ross Street. "I was born at 1 Hope Street and my father was a painter and decorator. I was one of eight, my mother having five boys

before she had me." She went to St Philip's Girls' School in Catherine Street and then was apprenticed to George Stoakley, the bookbinder in Green Street. "I worked there till war broke out, then I was of an age when we girls had to go into the factories. I went to a brush factory in St Albans." What was life like when she was a little girl? Hard times. "My father earned 35 shillings a week. He used to do a ceiling for 2s 6d and paper a room for 5 shillings. I have just had my front painted and it cost £90!" When her father was working up by the Men's Institute in East Road, Mrs Bell took him his dinner. "He'd pay me threepence a week for that. I used to run all the way from home with a little basket with a skewer through the top, and try not to spill the gravy." On the allotments where the council houses are now, Mrs Bell's father kept pigs. "He had 100 pigs once. He used to sell them to the butcher as he had to make money somehow. My father was a rare one. At night-time he would sit in the kitchen and mend all our shoes with a nice bit of leather that he had bought for sixpence. You never saw any of us children with run-down shoes, nor my mother." The customers queued up for meat at Bell's shop. "I did the booking for him. During the war I had to do all the ration books. One time I had 1,000 to count, and ended up weighing them!" After that she always weighed them! When William Bell died, the shop became successively a television and wireless repair shop, a toy shop, and a greengrocer's and general store. Recently it has sold second-hand clothes, but six weeks ago it opened again as a greengrocer's and general stores under the name of Peter Hinde.

Mrs Daisy Chapman, a near neighbour of Bert Forsdyke, is another well-known inhabitant of Ross Street. In her time, to quote the maestro Forsdyke, "she was a fine bowls player". George Goodyear, a retired railwayman of 96 who lives at Nutbourne Cottages, Ross Street, is a familiar figure on the recreation ground, where he exercises his brown and white spaniel four times a day. Bert Forsdyke's father Arthur George Forsdyke was a carpenter who helped to build houses in Ross Street in 1910. When the first world war broke out he constructed huts for the army. In 1914 Bert was ten and still at school, but he worked hard in his spare time to earn money for the family. He did a paper round in the week, and was a butcher's boy on Friday and Saturday. In the dark evenings in the ill-lit streets (Ross Street only had a couple of lights, which the lamplighter controlled), the paper boys cycled round with an old candle lamp. As a butcher's boy, Bert worked from 6 p.m. to 11 p.m. every Friday after he had done his paper round. On the Saturday he was back at the butcher's at 8 a.m. and worked until 11 p.m., preparing orders and then delivering them. "After that, we had to collect the money because no one was paid until 8 p.m. on a Saturday night. Perhaps we would get a farthing or a halfpenny tip. My wages were 1s 6d." His two elder brothers worked as grocer's assistants. On Sundays, Bert was a choirboy in the Wesleyan Chapel at the top of Hemingford Road, now the Romsey Mill. He was paid a shilling a quarter for his singing, and fined a penny if he didn't attend. He started his full-time working life in 1918, when he went to work on the railways. "I earned 7s 6d a week, which was 1s 6d more than the other boys because I was a competent shorthand typist. I worked for the Great Eastern Railways from 8 a.m. until 8 p.m. six days a week. In those days we used to get three days holiday a year." He worked as a clerk for British Rail for 46 years, and finished up as head of the Traffic Managers Works Accident and General Section. He has lived in Ross Street since 1936.

One of the strengths of Ross Street is the community ties which bind the residents together in a neighbourly way. These links, built over the years, are a positive force in this heart of Romsey.

13 Catherine Street

8 October 1981

The skylark once soared in the fields down Catherine Street, off Mill Road, and when, some 70 years ago, the boys there wanted to earn a penny or two, they'd catch the greenfinches and the goldfinches feeding on the thistles and sell them for pocket money. "We used to sell those greenfinches – a penny for a cock bird, a halfpenny for the hen." Edgar Nordon, a retired engine driver and prize fuchsia grower, one of the oldest inhabitants of Catherine Street, recalls rustic Romsey. He was born at no. 94, the house which he later bought from his father for £200, where in the narrow garden he still cultivates a few luscious ruby and garnet coloured fuchsias, and treasures a station lamp from Newport, which he lights up at night like a beacon at the end of the path. No. 132 was the last house in the street then, and a hedge was the demarcation line between the street and the fields beyond. "My father used to keep pigs over that hedge. Everybody kept a pig in those days."

Catherine Street, originally spelt Catharine and probably named after the wife of the local builder, Thoday, who gave his name to a parallel street, is a Victorian street nearly 100 years old. It has its Alice and Jubilee Cottages in the terrace row. In 1884 there were about 20 families living there, many of the menfolk being employed on the railway. There was George Blake, the engine cleaner, at no. 5, and next door, Samuel Potter, the coal porter. Frederick Huckle, the shunter, lived next to George Helmer, the railway servant. Charles Few, the engine driver, and Charles Ambrose, the railway labourer, were further down the street. One of the first shops in Catherine Street must have been The Catherine Wheel, a baker's and grocer's run by Edward J. Mason. The railway community of Catherine Street was beginning to evolve.

One of the very first inhabitants was John Merryweather, described in the 1884 street directory as a labourer. He was the father of 88-year-old Edward Merryweather, a retired railway telecommunications worker, who has lived on his own since his wife died, at 121 Catherine Street. "I was born in the second house down from the pub," he said. The pub is the Jubilee Tavern, built in Jubilee Year, 1887

(the same year as the Empress in Thoday Street). Like Edgar Nordon, Edward Merryweather can recall the early days in Catherine Street. "People used to go shooting duck when the fields at the end of the street were flooded. The fields belonged to Pink, the cattle dealer." Clearly Catherine Street was a street of birds. They were the patches of colour, like the flowers in the back gardens, in an externally drab street. Mr Merryweather remembers that a gamekeeper lived at no. 126. "He kept coloured birds in his back yard." He is listed in the directory as William Cator, living in a house called Rye Cottage. Cowsheds in Thoday Street were a magnet for the mischievous boys of Catherine Street. Mr Merryweather: "We used to go down the passage leading through into Thoday Street and poke those cows with a stick. Away would go the old milk!" On another occasion young Merryweather and his pals felt the policeman's strap when they were caught pinching carrots from a local allotment.

Nos. 126a, b and c, three houses with bay windows and a patch of front garden where a hydrangea blooms – the only front gardens in Catherine Street – stand on the site of a slaughterhouse, which, says Mr Merryweather, belonged to a man called Swan. The bay-windowed houses have escapist names – Clacton, Melrose and Glenville. No. 120 was once a launderette. It is now divided into flats. Further up, nos. 114 and 116 were built for Reginald Wright, on land which he had bought, to his own design. He and his wife moved into no. 114 when they were married in 1917; they let no. 116. Their son Mr Eric Wright, of 26 Catherine Street, was born in no. 114 and lived there until his own marriage in 1967. The house remained in his family's possession until 1976.

Children have been coming to school in Catherine Street since 1886 when the school was first built. It was originally known as St Barnabas' School because of its connection with St Barnabas' Church. It later became St Philip's Church School. To begin with it was for infants and junior girls, and originally it had only one schoolroom. It was enlarged in 1887 and between 1888 and 1894. In 1894 another school, for boys only, was opened in Ross Street. St Philip's School was overcrowded in the early 1900s: in 1911

Terrace houses in Catherine Street

it had 870 children, compared with 430 in 1948. Now it is a junior school with 120 children, scheduled to be rebuilt on land in Vinery Road when what administrators call the due process is complete.

The school's first log book, which is kept in the County Record Office at Shire Hall, certifies that the school opened on Monday, 29 March 1886. Miss Eleanor Robson was the headmistress. The log says: "107 children were admitted in the morning, and ten in the afternoon." An entry for May 21 for that year says: "Reading and arithmetic of the fourth class is still very weak. Several of the children over seven do not know their letters." For a special recitation in 1888, the children learned great chunks of poetry by heart. One grade learned 100 lines of Scott's "Lady of the Lake". Another class committed 50 lines of Shakespeare's *King John* to memory. Throughout the early days of the school, attendance was very poor, as repeated reference to absenteeism in the log makes clear. 28 June 1886: "Poor attendance on Friday afternoon owing to the Fair, only 106 were present. 106 were absent." 8 January 1901: "Attendance very poor. A great deal of illness in the neighbourhood. Weather also bad."

Into the 1920s now, and the log stresses the importance of patriotism. Empire Day was an important occasion each year and St Philip's School joined in the celebrations. On 25 May 1921, the log records that a service was held at 9.05 a.m. in St Philip's Church. "The preacher was the Rev. E.P. Hindley. In the school ordinary lessons were suspended and a special programme of folk dancing and patriotic songs and action songs, including an Empire Pageant, an address by Mrs Bethune Baker on Empire Making and concluding with saluting the flag and God Save the King, was gone through in the presence of a good audience of parents and friends of the school." On 31 May 1921 the children had a half-day's holiday to celebrate the visit of the Prince of Wales to Cambridge. The log reports: "The Prince of Wales visited Cambridge. The children left school at 10 a.m. and walked in twos to opposite the Botanical Gardens on Trumpington Road where they were lined up to welcome the Prince. There was a holiday in the afternoon." On 14 October that year another half-day's holiday was given to the children "owing to the visit of their Majesties The King and Queen to Cambridge". At the beginning of the war the school was frequently disturbed by the air raid siren. On 21 January 1941 the log records "Tuesday: A day much interrupted by the siren. Two periods were spent in the shelters in the

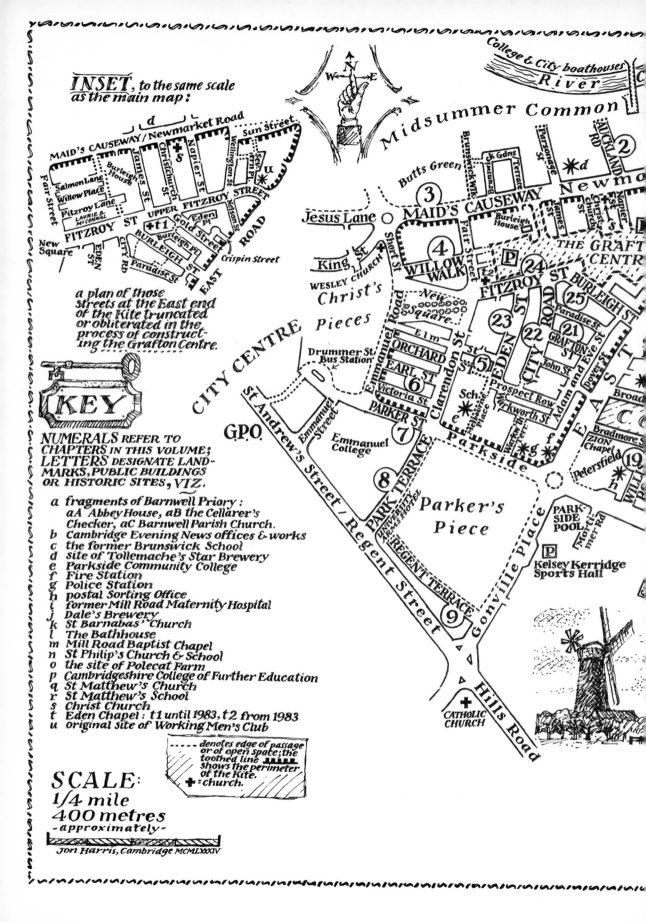

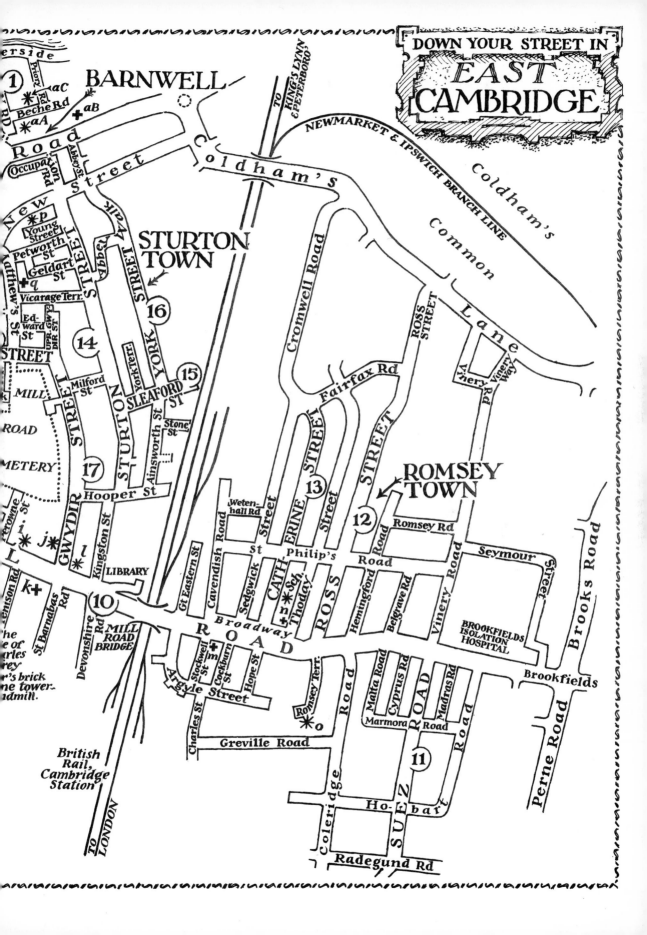

BARNWELL

①

*aC
Priory Rd
Beche Rd
+aB
*aA

Riverside

New Road

Occupation Rd

Abbey St

Street Walk

STURTON
TOWN

Coldham's

TO KING'S LYNN & PETERBORO'

NEWMARKET & IPSWICH BRANCH LINE

Coldham's

Common

Lane

*p
Young Street
Petworth St
Geldart St
+q
Vicarage Terr.
Edward St

UPR. GWYDIR ST.

Street Walk

Abbey

York Street

⑯

⑭

Matthew's St

STREET

MILL

ROAD

CEMETERY

Milford St
Sleaford St
Ainsworth St
Stone St
York Terr.

STURTON

⑰

⑮

Hooper St

STREET

GWYDIR

Browne's St
i
*j
l
Kingston St
LIBRARY
Atkinson Rd
k+

⑩

St Barnabas Rd
Devonshire Rd
MILL
ROAD
BRIDGE

the
site of
Charles
Grey
Grey's brick
stone tower
windmill.

Gt Eastern St

Cavendish Road

Wetenhall Rd

Sedgwick St

CATHERINE STREET

St Philip's Sch.
*n
+
Thoday

ROSS STREET

Cromwell Road

Fairfax Rd

ROSS STREET

Vinery Rd

Vinery Way

ROMSEY
TOWN

⑬

⑫

Romsey Rd

Romsey Rd

Romsey Road

Hemingford Rd

Belgrave Rd

Vinery Road

Seymour Street

Brooks Road

BROOKFIELDS
ISOLATION
HOSPITAL

Brookfields

Perne Road

Broadway

ROAD

Stockwell St
*m
Cockburn St
Hope St

Charles St
Argyle Street
Romsey Terr.
*o

Greville Road

British
Rail,
Cambridge
Station

TO LONDON

Coleridge Road

Malta Road
Cyprus Rd
Marmora Road
Madras Rd

SUEZ ROAD

ROAD

⑪

Hobart Road

Radegund Rd

Mr Charles Plumb with old bottles at the off licence in Catherine Street

morning and two periods in the afternoon." When the school reopened for the year on 7 September 1942, 22 London evacuees were absorbed into it and a London County Council teacher added to the staff. One striking feature of the design of St Philip's School is its windows. They are built high up – to stop the children from seeing out and being distracted!

Many people in Romsey Town remember French's, the corn merchants, on the corner of Catherine Street and Mill Road. George French, the corn and seed merchant, was in business there, and at 173 East Road, from the 1890s for many

years. Bert Forsdyke of 157 Ross Street remembers watching the bags of grain being taken up by hoist to the loft above. The hoist has gone now. "My father used to get his oats, bran and pollard for his rabbits and chickens there. There were three steps leading up to the entrance, which was on Mill Road."

Next door to French's was Bailey and Tebbitt's off-licence, managed by Mr Charles Plumb, who has been in the drinks business for 30 years. "When French's retired they sold the business, including the off-licence premises, to Dale's, the brewery." Mr Plumb started work as a driver for Wadsworth's, the mineral water people. During the war he transferred to Baldrys and worked for them for 47 years, driving in a radius of 30 miles around Cambridge. "When I first started, lemonades were ninepence a dozen." Two interesting bygones are on display at the off-licence. One is a lemonade bottle with an intriguing stopper – a marble that kept the bottle airtight until it was released by pressure from the opener. Once released, the marble bobbed about in the neck of the bottle. These old lemonade bottles were popular as money boxes. Mr Plumb's other bygone is a 1902 ginger beer bottle made by the Sawston Aerated Water Company. Mr Plumb is helped in the off-licence by his son-in-law, Mr M.D. Nicolls, who spoke about the days when the men of Romsey Town – "Red Russia they used to call it" – were involved with the railway. "Over here it was nearly all railway workers, more than 70 per cent I should say. There were many more engines than there are now. You no longer see the driver walking up the street and over the bridge in his smart uniform with his little black box. They were big men like the engines they drove. They wore small donkey coats, well-washed overalls and black horse-skin caps."

Few Cambridge streets can now boast of having a first-rate butcher and a fishmonger. Catherine Street has both. P. Hunt, the butcher's that used to be a greengrocer's and general store at one time, is well patronised. Across at no. 71, Edward and Joan Hammond have been running the fish and chip shop for 34 years. When the shop first started it belonged to Ralph Goodrum, Mrs Hammond's brother-in-law. Mrs Hammond and her sister, who married Ralph Goodrum, were daughters of a railwayman. It is appropriate that Edward Hammond is a good fisherman and a member of the Cambridge Albion Society.

Among the businesses in Catherine Street today are a flooring company, the Castle Flooring Company, at no. 68, premises which in recent times have housed a greengrocer and a night club. In 1895 Miss Fanny Few ran a drapery and general stores there. Her father was Charles Few the engine driver. Further down, at no. 103, where W.G. Undrill, the upholsterers and polishers, are now, there used to be the firm of J.R. Bennett and Sons, builders, contractors and undertakers. Edgar Nordon went to work for Bennetts when he left school at 14. His job was to drive a pony and cart loaded with ammunition boxes made by Bennetts over to Chivers at Histon, who filled them with tins of jam that were then sent to the soldiers at the Front. "I was paid twopence an hour for the work," he said.

Catherine Street is included in the Romsey General Improvement Area. One of the street representatives for the G.I.A. is Mrs Kate Ducker at no. 7, who is responsible for nos. 1–33 and 26–28, and attends committee meetings to discuss improvement plans. Her own job, like that of several other residents in the street, is in publishing. At the moment she is working for Chadwyck-Healey Ltd, checking Parliamentary papers of 100 years ago – papers reflecting living conditions and social problems which were not uncommon in the Catherine Street of that period.

14 Sturton Street

29 March–19 April 1984

Sturton Street is by definition the heart of Sturton Town – that part of Cambridge which links East Road with the Mill Road railway bridge. A long, narrow street of terraced houses developed in the 1870s and 1880s to house a growing population of railway workers and other employees, Sturton Street today is also the home of young dons, nurses, writers and professional people, members of an expanding population in a city where housing is expensive and scarce.

Just as many roads and streets in Cambridge are named after the *eminences grises* of the colleges which own the land on which they have been developed, so Sturton Street commemorates one of the town's civic worthies. Joseph Sturton, retail chemist, alderman and mayor, bought a large parcel of land in the Mill Road–Newmarket Road district, originally part of the Barnwell Fields, later the Panton estate, and developed it with houses for working-class families.

For a portrait of Mr Sturton we can do no better than refer to the *Cambridge Graphic* for 5 January 1901, which gives a whimsical account of the great man in its series of "Cambridge Sketches": "It was in the second year of the reign of Queen Victoria that Mr Sturton came to Cambridge and founded the business in Fitzroy Street that is now carried on by members of his family. Fortune favoured him, as it always does favour industry and sagacity, and the business became firmly established. It has been said that the difference between the successful and the unsuccessful man is that the one has embraced his opportunities, the other has not. Mr Sturton's opportunities of benefiting at once himself and his town came when he was enabled to purchase land on the north side of Cambridge, then open fields, now thickly covered with houses. Mr Sturton had the foresight to recognise the possibilities that were in this land, and he had the courage of his convictions. In the result his sagacity has been magnificently vindicated. He bought extensively, and when the time came, he sold."

The manner of his selling deserves, however, to be specially emphasised, says the *Graphic*. "The policy that is generally pursued by those who have bought land that is suitable for building is to hold it as long as possible, and then to sell it for as high a price as can be obtained. But Mr Sturton had the enterprise and the public spirit to apply to the sale of his land the principle of small profits and quick returns. Therein he took what proved a wise course for himself, and at the same time he conferred a public benefit." What Sturton did was this: he became a speculator with a strain of philanthropy. When he sold his land and properties, he allowed the occupier-purchasers to make repayments for their houses over a series of years, which meant, as the *Graphic* put it, that "many to whom otherwise it would have been impossible, were enabled to become possessed not only of houses but of freeholds of their own." Joseph Sturton was an active local politician for many years. He was a member of the first County Council, and for several years he sat on the Cambridge Board of Guardians. He was a devout man, too, and a generous supporter of the Baptist Chapel in Tenison Road.

It was in the early 1870s that Sturton began to put Sturton Street on the map. By 1874, 34 houses had been built, including Haylock Cottages (a terrace of five houses) and Troy Cottages (consisting of a bakery and a public house, the City Arms). The early occupants were bootmakers, tailors, carpenters and gardeners, some of the hundreds of artisans who were to inhabit this part of Cambridge in the last years of the 19th century. The street also had its miller, a man called Angiel who lived in Haylock Cottages (sounds like a Hardy novel). Among the first houses were nos. 57, 59 and 61. On 28 May 1981, Miss Daphne Foreman, of 61 Sturton Street, wrote to the *Weekly News* to say that she hoped I would one day write about Sturton Street, and included some interesting details. The deeds to her house show the "proposed roadway" where Sturton Street now runs, and nos. 57, 59 and 61 marked on a little sketch. "We may be the original or at least some of the first of the artisans' terrace houses in Sturton Street, although there are some attractive Victorian villas lower down in the street which must have been suburban properties," she said. At one time 63 Sturton Street was a blacksmith's, and next to it is no. 63a, a house built into the actual smithy. The lintel of the forge entrance can be seen in the brickwork from Miss Foreman's garden.

One of the first tradesmen in Sturton Street was Henry Cable, the baker, born in Halstead in 1840. He founded his bread-making business at no. 9 in 1888. Before that he was the first Co-op baker in Cambridge. He lived then with his wife and three children in James Street, near the bakery. The Co-op apparently wanted him not only to bake the bread, but also to push a hand-cart around the streets selling it. He told them he was a master baker and refused to push a cart. They bowed to the pressure by buying him a horse-drawn van, according to a biography in the Cambridgeshire Collection. When he set up in business on his own in the rented shop and bakehouse in Sturton Street, he had to be up before five each morning to make the bread from dough which had been left to rise in the troughs overnight. He called that "setting the sponge". Everything was done by hand. The oven held 25 stones of bread, eight loaves to a stone. The usual daily amount baked was two and a half oven loads or 500 loaves, including farmhouse and cottage loaves, rolls and twists, tins and sandwiches and some Hovis loaves. At Easter time he made hot cross buns, and at Christmas he allowed his customers to use his oven to cook their Christmas dinners.

While the family minded the shop, Henry would go out with a horse and cart and sell his bread from Abbey Road to Brookside and "over the line" – over Mill Road bridge. When his son, Frederick, married and had children of his own, one of them, Henry's grandson Frank, went into partnership with Henry. He remembered Henry reading his newspaper and laughing over man's first attempts to fly – "Look at this, boy, they've stayed up for a whole two minutes – they'll never do it." Together Frank and Henry watched the first balloon ascent from Cambridge from a yard behind the Bird in Hand public house in Newmarket Road. In 1909, Frank Cable took over the business. His son, Robert Cable, of 16 Sunnyside, Cambridge, remembers that his father's first ton of coal for the business cost 16 shillings and he was given a shilling back for paying up promptly. Next door to the bakery in Sturton Street was the Co-op stable yard, where 40 horses were stabled and looked after by Mr Tom Blazeley. "He did a fine job," said Mr Cable, "for the horses always looked very well groomed and smartly turned out."

The Sturton Street Methodist Church, built in 1875 and rebuilt in 1954 after wartime bomb damage, was the first place of worship in this densely

Joseph Sturton at the age of 88, a picture from the Cambridge Graphic *of 5 January 1901*

populated part of the town. Today it still has a small but loyal following – a congregation of 25 to 30 in the morning and 12 to 15 in the evening, according to the senior steward, Mr Jack Langford, of 94 Lovell Road, who has attended the chapel since the age of seven. His wife Hilda (née Endersby) can beat that – she was first taken to chapel by her mother at the age of three weeks, her father being a trustee.

The first superintendent of the chapel more than 100 years ago was the Rev. W. Rudd, a superannuated minister who was successful in establishing the

Twenty years ago – Sturton Street in 1964. Externally the street has not changed much

chapel in the community. The jubilee souvenir handbook of the Primitive Methodist Chapel, as it was then called, published in 1925, gives an account of those early days, quoting an old scholar of the Sunday School, Robert Pilgrim, whose recollections tell us about both the chapel and Sturton Street.

"My earliest recollections of Sturton Street are that the roads were not made up and that as a child I had to step on stones and bricks to keep clear of the mud and pools of water. My father and mother then occupied the house no. 63, opposite the chapel, and no. 63a was at that time a gateway with a loft above." He refers to this entrance and loft because, before the chapel was built, this place was used by the Primitive Methodists of the district as a place of worship. "Rev. Tongue and Rev. Bell used to preach here. While this place was used, the people who attended brought their chairs and hymn books and some kind friend brought a small harmonium to lead the singing." Of the Rev. Rudd, Robert Pilgrim writes: "I remember he had a beautiful plant in his window in Kingston Street, and my father admired it and said he would like a cutting. Mr Rudd referred him to the good old Book as follows: 'Thou shalt not covet thy neighbour's goods.' My father did not get a cutting."

Robert Pilgrim and his sister were among the first pupils at the Sunday School, where nearly all the teachers were workers on the Great Eastern Railway. He had to help carry the banner of the school through the streets on treat days. He recalls that hymn singing played an important part in the services in the early days, one hymn in particular being a great favourite:

> Once I heard a sound at my heart's dark door
> And was roused from the slumber of sin,
> It was Jesus knocked, He had knocked before,
> Now I said "Blessed Master come in".

"The inhabitants of Sturton Street some considerable distance away must have heard us singing that hymn many times," he writes. "We put some go into it!"

As the congregations at the new chapel grew, the Sunday School, in particular, had difficulty in accommodating all its pupils. A special schoolroom was built next to the chapel in 1901, but 20 years later when they were even more short of space, it was decided that an Army hut should be bought for use as extra school premises. In August 1941, a high-explosive bomb partially destroyed the chapel. Some attempt was made to repair the building, but it was unsatisfactory and services were conducted in the nearby assembly hall. The present chapel was built for £6,000 in 1954; its foundation stone was laid by the then Master of Downing College, Professor Sir Lionel Whitby.

Today a street of burgeoning window-boxes, stylish house conversions and housing developments such as Linnett House and Kerridge Close, Sturton Street has become a desirable area, not least because the house prices are within the reach of first-time buyers, but also because it is within easy reach of the City centre. This used to be the street of the engine drivers, the L.N.E.R. shunters, the wiremen and fitters, as well as the mattress maker, the billiard table repairer, the corn merchant's carman and the public disinfector, to name some of the occupants of the many houses in Sturton Street in its early years. There were several dairymen in the street. On the west side at no. 89 was William Biggs; Mrs Sheila Campbell now lives in the attractively transformed and enlarged house with its big garden. And then further down at no. 141 lived Ernest Saggers, whose wife was the local nurse. This was in the mid-1920s, but some ten years earlier there was another dairy in Sturton Street, a farm called Summerfield's between the junctions with Geldart Street and Petworth, Young and New Streets. And about ten years before that, as Fred Boreham of Lichfield Road tells me, "my uncle Fred (Fiddler) Boreham kept a small herd of milking cows in the yards of nos. 93 and 95. At that time all milkmen were suspected of watering down their milk, hence the nickname." Mr Boreham was born at no. 93 in 1910. "My father worked at Warboys Brewery as a drayman and served in the evenings at the bottle and jug, so when my uncle Fred died at an early age the nickname

The Primitive Methodist Chapel in Sturton Street. The first chapel (1875) was damaged by a bomb on 29 August 1941; the new chapel was opened in 1954

rubbed off on him." At that time no. 89 was a wheelwright's yard owned by John Miller; Mr Boreham remembers him doing his deliveries by bicycle, trundling the repaired wheels beside him.

Many Cambridge residents have rich memories of their childhoods in the Sturton Street of pre-war days. Mr Leslie Wallis of Neville Road, whose family lived at no. 175, opposite the City Arms, sent me his recollections: "Mrs Speechley (landlady of the City Arms) was an excellent pianist who was relief solo pianist at the Playhouse Cinema, Mill Road (now Tesco's). Many times I've heard her playing in the pub saloon bar as the sounds wafted into Sturton Street – we had Chopin and popular songs of the day, which everyone enjoyed." Mr Wallis' uncle Mr Newman ran one of the three corner grocery shops in the street. "Here one could buy anything from sweets to groceries, pickles, jams, biscuits and vegetables. Jams and pickles were not sold in one-pound jars but loose from a large earthenware jar. One took along an old cup which was duly weighed on the big scales – then a large wooden spoon was produced, which was used to dig out the jam or pickles to be weighed in the cup.

"Across the road towards Milford Street was a small factory known as the Tin Factory, at nos. 152–156. Throughout the working day a noisy clatter, din and rattle was produced, and pots and pans, kettles

An interior view of the converted Old Bakehouse

and various household articles were the end result. It was mainly staffed by girls. We always stopped to peer into this fascinating place where the doors were usually left open. On the other side of the road was Mr Ernest Saggers' small shop. He sold rabbits and fowls and he would soon skin and cut up a rabbit for about one shilling. I have many happy memories of the 1920s at Sturton Street, of the street lamplighter, the horse-drawn carts of the tradesmen who called, the street organ grinder, exchanging glass jars for windmills from a trader with a barrow and so many more. We had just enough to live on in those days, no luxuries but we were happy."

Miss D.M. Maltby of Mortlock Avenue attended the Sturton Street National School at no. 57 (now Stockbridge's workshop) during the first world war, where the head teacher Miss Bryant gave her pupils some ineradicable memories: "She wore a long trench raincoat reaching to the top of her button boots, summer and winter, and strode along to the school with her furled man-sized umbrella. When the children happened to meet her outside the

Henry Cable outside his bakery in Sturton Street in the early 1900s

school, the boys had to salute and the girls had to curtsey. Woe betide anybody who infringed that rule. A few hard smacks on each hand soon put that right. Also in those days the girls mostly wore white starched pinafores, and the stiffer they were starched the posher you were – and being a spoiled only child I was one of the posh ones. Every morning we had to say our two times table up to six times, in a sing-song fashion, but how it stuck. Incidentally, the pinafores came in very useful, because if you so much as glanced round in class, out you had to come, go into the corner of the room, put your pinafore over your head and stand there, until the powers that be in the awesome shape of Miss Bryant told you to return to your seat."

One of the oldest living connections with the street is that provided by Miss Eileen Runham of St Philip's Road, granddaughter of Mr and Mrs Warboys, who owned Warboys Brewery opposite the end of Milford Street from its beginnings in the 1870s until 1906. A brewery until the late twenties, by 1931 it had become the premises of a motor coach firm. The Warboys lived at no. 120, next to the brewery yard and stables.

Of all the conversions of property in this area from commercial to residential use, as the estate agents say, the one that would win my unofficial

By the light of a flickering flame – Bessie Thurbon lighting one of her gas lamps

accolade for ingenuity is that of the property called the Old Bakehouse next to 117 Sturton Street, built in 1884 by one James Burford. Local lore has it that baking stopped here in about 1954 "when the price of flour went up". Formerly 1a Milford Street, the property with flour loft and baker's oven and later a warehouse had become derelict when an enterprising New Zealand girl called Andy Laing spotted it three years ago. She and her young son were homeless at the time and had very limited resources. Friends were aghast at her plans to convert the Old Bakehouse, and building society and local officials clearly had the business equivalent of sleepless nights over the whole project. But they helped her, and with the aid of a good architect and builder, plus that key ingredient – planning permission – she achieved her extensive alterations, fashioning a bedroom for herself out of what used to be the baker's oven (after 32 tons of brickwork had been removed), and a large well-lit living area in what must have been the old flour loft. The interior brick-

work has been sandblasted and family life upstairs focusses round the hearth. It is all very snug and, as Andy Laing says, "best of all is when we have a fire and can watch the snow landing on the skylights". The long room of the Old Bakehouse has added a new dimension to Sturton Street. The one drawback is a total absence of garden, but the view of other people's green-fingered efforts in adjacent gardens in Milford Street and Gwydir Street is aesthetically pleasing.

There can be few streets in England, let alone Cambridge, where you will find gas lighting in one house, and the latest in Design Centre fittings in the next (or next but few . . .). That is Sturton Street for you. Gentrification is taking place at a rate – with houses on sale at £28,000. "It's all you can afford on a University lecturer's pay," they say, but the traditional values as well as the traditional house fittings remain in this mixed but very neighbourly community, where even the local cats get a good look in. Retired college gardeners and servants seem to rub shoulders quite amicably with the exuberant activists who have moved into the street and become involved with local politics (Sturton Street is part of the St Matthew's Improvement Area); CND (its Press Officer Eric van Tassel lives at 4 Oswald Terrace); and Animal Aid, chairperson Joan Court of 74 Sturton Street, a much-travelled woman whose zest for life and attitudes on contentious issues owe much to the example and inspiration of Gandhi – "my first cultural hero". She was working in Calcutta as a midwife for the Quakers during Independence in 1947 and actually witnessed the riots and saw the flags come down. (Are "Jewel in the Crown" addicts listening?)

But the point is, the old Sturton Street and the old values survive. It's to do with dignity, self respect and independence, not to mention neighbourly tact and concern, that one old lady (and there may be several others in the area) is still living without electricity, a bathroom or hot running water in Sturton Street. Nobody has forced change on her, preferring to leave her in surroundings and conditions which many would find quaint and Dickensian but which have been familiar to her for a lifetime. For Bessie Thurbon, home in Sturton Street is an extension of herself. It is where she was born in 1906 and for years it was the family home. And by the light of the flickering gas lamp – mantles are 80*p* each and may last her a year if she is careful – she tells her story. Afterwards we go into the kitchen by torchlight and Miss Thurbon lights another candle. There is only gaslight in her sitting and living room and in one bedroom upstairs. The other rooms and the landing and cellar are unlit.

The house, she says, and the adjacent house were built by a Miss Hannah Lawrie as a laundry. Miss Thurbon's house was the actual laundry and had a 10-gallon copper in the kitchen. "There used to be a big room which ran over my kitchen and the kitchen of the house next door. That was the ironing room. The wide passage between the two houses was the place where the handcart was kept. It was in this cart that the baskets of clothes were brought to the laundry. The women who worked in the laundry used to earn 1s 6d for a day's work, however long that might be, together with a glass of beer and a piece of bread and cheese." The casks of beer were kept in the cellar – which looked very deep by the light of the torch. Miss Lawrie's brother, William, described in the 1881 street directory as an army pensioner, lived with his sister next door. He had been blinded in combat – which could have been in the Crimean War (my guess).

The Thurbon family moved into Sturton Street from Rivar Place. Miss Thurbon's father, William, was a coffin maker who worked for Merry, the undertaker in Abbey Walk. He was the eldest of eight children, and was apprenticed as a coffin maker in London at the age of nine and a half. For many years after he married, he continued to work in London, coming down on Sundays to visit his wife and family. But, his daughter recalls, he was taken ill one day in Devonshire Road (presumably en route to the station). After that he ceased travelling to London and started work with Mr Merry instead. When Miss Thurbon was a child she caught scarlet fever from the man who used to drive the local fever cart. "This man used to work at Merry's, too, and he had a habit of hanging his coat up on top of Dad's. That was how I caught scarlet fever. My uncle who was working at the Isolation Hospital at Oakington told my mother how to nurse me and a sheet dipped in disinfectant was hung over the bedroom door." Miss Thurbon was incarcerated upstairs for eight weeks and away from school for four months. Her father, clearly, was a popular local figure. After school the boys from St Matthew's in York Street used to call at Merry's to watch him work, and two little evacuee girls from London told him, "if ever the war is over and we go back to London, we shall want you to make our coffins".

But no mention of the kindly Miss Thurbon, who was a teacher at St Matthew's Sunday School for 50 years, would be complete without reference to her cats. She is known far and wide as a lover of cats. A favourite, Hobby, has recently died, but friends have presented her with Honey. There is a cats' graveyard in the garden at the back and among old friends buried there is a special favourite, whom her father called "Monty". A stalwart member of the local Cats Collective, Miss Thurbon and her neighbour Jenny Sherlock find and feed lost cats. There are three colonies of local "lost" neutered cats which are fed by them and another friend, Hilda, from Gwydir Street. One of the most recent recruits to the Cat Colony is Thomas, the cat who was left behind when the maternity hospital moved from Mill Road to its new home, the Rosie. (Sturton Street is also a popular area with nurses; there are several living in the street.)

If cats meet round at Bessie's, as Miss Thurbon is affectionately known, so the humans congregate at Pawley's, the popular local butcher, described by local residents as the big social centre of the neighbourhood. The shop was started in 1895 by Mr G. Sansom and Mr Swann – Swann and Sansom, it was called. It then passed to Mr Sansom's son, the East Anglian racing cyclist T.S. Sansom, well known in the 1920s. Finally, Mr R. Sansom, grandson of the founder, took it on. Now it is Pawley's.

Opposite Pawley's is Oswald Terrace – a row of "seaside" villas built in 1906, it is said, by a builder

Gillian Mann and Michael Lapidge at no. 143 Sturton Street

Charles Kerridge Jnr driving along in a Daimler with the architect, Mr Keefer, who designed his house at Lordship Close, Stapleford

called Oswald. "The houses were set back two feet from the road. The bay windows were constructed on the cheap as there is no bay to sit in. They were self-conscious and up-market for the time," says Eric van Tassel, who lives at 4 Oswald Terrace with his wife Jane. They both work for Cambridge University Press, and are both active members of CND. Every month they distribute 400 posters.

Building skills and a clever eye for detail were involved in one of Sturton Street's most dramatic conversions. Five years ago two University lecturers (both medievalists) enlarged and re-created no. 143 by joining together nos. 143 and 145. The latter property was formerly a bakery (1935), and before that, in the 1920s, the premises of a mineral water manufacturer. Michael Lapidge and Gillian Mann have made themselves a splendid den, fashioning studies in the west-facing eaves which command perhaps unexpected views of the pinnacles of King's College Chapel. There are two staircases and quite a feeling of spaciousness about their home, which is

one of the very interesting examples of innovative house adaptation in this rapidly changing, but still socially cohesive part of Cambridge.

Sited now in smart new offices, formerly premises belonging to the Co-op, the building firm of Kerridge was started in 1880 by Charles Kerridge and George Shaw. They married sisters, daughters of James Footer of Exning, a builder with whom they both worked until they came to Cambridge. George Shaw lived at Burwell and Charles Kerridge came from Walsham-le-Willows; they founded their partnership shortly after coming to Cambridge. In Sturton Street they lived at nos. 26 and 28, with an archway between the houses. Later, according to notes made by Charles Kerridge's daughter, Miss Ada Kerridge, in 1952, no. 26 was occupied by Mr Davis, a clerk, while no. 28 was made into offices in 1896.

Work began in a small way, but the business became renowned for reliability. Mr Shedd was the first carpenter foreman at the works, and Harry Ransom the first employee. "Kerridge and Shaw worked hard and were asked to tender for larger jobs. They prospered," wrote Miss Kerridge. "Strikes occurred, but Father, nothing daunted, drove employees into the country to a job, rising at six o'clock each morning and fetching them at night." The Cambridge building industry's first machinery was installed in their works about 1892. Among the places built by the firm in the early years was Colchester Town Hall, and they also made additions to Melton Lunatic Asylum, then so called. Miss Kerridge recalled that Charles Kerridge's son, Charles Jnr, lived for a time at Woodbridge while supervising the Melton job, and it was here that he met his wife, mother of the late Alderman Kelsey Kerridge.

Charles Kerridge Jnr reformed the company in 1914. Charles had a brother called William, who died in an accident on a building site. The firm built several hotels on the east coast, including the Grand Hotel, Southwold, and the Bath Hotel at Felixstowe. They constructed St Andrew's Street Baptist Church and the adjacent Fire Station in Cambridge, and built a new shop for Jermyn's of King's Lynn after theirs was destroyed by fire. In 1903 they built Laurie and McConnal in Fitzroy Street; the building is still a popular landmark. The Medical School in Downing Street, also built by Kerridge, was opened by King Edward VII. Miss Kerridge preserved the family's invitations to seats in the Downing Site quadrangle and luncheon at King's College. They also did work at Bushy Royal Caledonian Orphanage, opened by Princess Beatrice, and many places in London, including additions to Westminster Training College and Greenwich Fire Station.

In the firm's archives is a copy of the working rules of the Cambridge District of the Association of Operative Plasterers. Workmen were paid by the hour. The present managing director is Mr Paul Kerridge, who remembers buying biscuits and cakes

Mr Paul Kerridge in his office in Sturton Street

at the old Co-op, now the firm's headquarters. Mr Kerridge has observed, and presided over, several business changes in the firm since it was sold to Matthews Holdings in 1973. Now the firm is once again controlled by a member of the Kerridge family, and Paul's son Kelsey is the fifth generation of Kerridges to be associated with it.

15 Sleaford Street

7 October 1982

Co-op milk floats and petrol tankers now rumble down the street where world-famous cricketer Jack Hobbs used to play with a cabbage stalk for a bat when he was a boy in the 1890s. He and his family – he had five brothers and six sisters – lived in a tiny terraced house in a lane called Rivar Place leading off Sleaford Street, deep in the heart of Sturton Town.

The houses in Sleaford Street and Rivar Place were built between 1874 and 1901 on land that Joseph Sturton had acquired (see Sturton Street). Like the building plots he sold off, the streets into which he divided the estate were narrow: Sleaford Street was 28 ft wide, neighbouring Ainsworth Street 30 ft.

Many plots in Sleaford Street were bought by Thomas Kingston, who built the first ten houses in the street and neighbouring Rivar Place. He built for himself the imposing residence called Rivar House or, less plausibly, Rivar Cottage, on the corner of the west side of Rivar Place. It is now the

Frank Hobbs and his wife Ellen with a photograph of his famous brother Jack

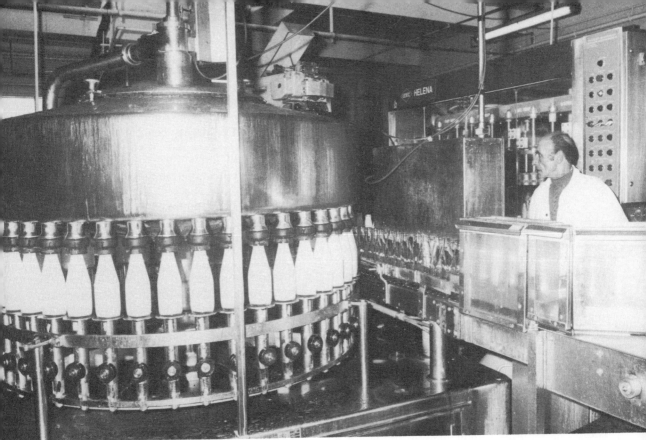

A lotta bottle . . . at the Co-op Dairy at the end of Sleaford Street

home of a group of self-employed builders. The parish rate book for 1877 shows that Thomas Kingston owned ten houses, one yard and a building in Sleaford Street. By 1880 he had acquired a stable as well. Thomas Kingston must have given his name to Kingston Street nearby, Sleaford Street is named after Sleaford in Lincolnshire; it is where the Sturton family came from. The name Rivar is a bit of a mystery – there is no place called Rivar listed in the *Gazetteer*. Could it have been a Kingston family name? His mother's maiden name, perhaps?

In 1874 there was just a builder living in Sleaford Street. His name was John L. Pate. Perhaps he was involved in the building of the local houses, for by 1878 part of Rivar Terrace had been built, and a baker called Edgar Tricker, a carpenter called William Loates, and Alfred Hardy, a painter, had moved in with their families. The register of baptisms for the parish of St Matthew records that on 28 April 1878 several children from Sleaford Street were christened in St James' Mission Church, a wooden building that stood on what is now waste ground on the corner of Ainsworth Street and Sleaford Street. John Pate's son, George Wesson Pate, was christened on that spring day together with two

of the Hardy children and five of baker Tricker's children. An evangelical clergyman must have whipped them all in! Later in the year, on 11 August 1878, Edgar Tricker the baker was christened at an adult baptism.

The Ordnance Survey map for 1886 shows Sleaford Street and Rivar Place to be nearly complete. The Geldart Inn, named after the former land-owner, had been built on the corner of Sleaford Street and Ainsworth Street, and on the north side Ebenezer Villas had been built between Sturton Street and York Terrace. Three houses on the opposite side of the street called Gladstone Terrace had been built in 1884. By 1887 several railway workers had moved into the street. There was Edward Morrell, a guard with the Great Eastern Railway, Charles Rickette, a railway servant, Robert Parr, an engine driver, Thomas Allen, a railway servant, and Charles Marshall, a servant with the G.E.R.

By the turn of the century, it is clear, there were three landlords in Sleaford Street. Thomas Kingston owned 12 houses in Rivar Place and 15 in Sleaford Street. E. Ledgar owned the three houses that made up Gladstone Terrace, and A.D. Atkin owned two houses in Sleaford Street. Of these, only Thomas Kingston lived in the street. Local people talk of the man they called "Miser" Kingston who lived at Rivar House with two dogs. He was a recluse with a long beard and local children were both intimidated by him and cheeky to him.

There is no blue plaque on the little back street cottage in Rivar Place where Sir Jack Hobbs lived as a boy after the family moved from Brewhouse Lane off Norfolk Terrace in the late 1880s or early 1890s. But people in the area know the family and remember the famous first son, who married local girl Ada Gates, whose father was a cobbler in Sleaford Street in the early 1900s. Jack Hobbs left home to start his career as a cricketer in 1899, so his youngest brother, Edward Frank Hobbs, who was born the following year, has few memories of his brother's early days. But as he told me at his home in 187 Sturton Street last week: "We knew he had made a name for himself, but we didn't think much of it." The Hobbs family's lifestyle was clearly not affected by the famous brother. The family continued to live in the area: Mrs Hobbs stayed on at 4 Rivar Place until 1934, brother Sidney opened the sports shop in Trinity Street, while Frank, who joined the army in 1919 and served in Gibraltar, India and China, returned to Cambridge to work for the Gas Company.

"At first it was pick and shovel work, then I became promoted to lamplighter. I went round the streets morning and night lighting the lamps and putting them out, until they got the clocks. My uniform was a peaked cap and overalls." Jack Hobbs' only surviving brother has clear memories of Sleaford Street in the early days. He remembers David Endersby, the general dealer and shopkeeper at 24 Sleaford Street, now Wingroves' general stores. "Mr Endersby sold practically everything." Mrs Fortin, who sold treacle and sweets at the shop on the corner of Sturton Street and Sleaford Street, was another popular shopkeeper with the Hobbs children.

David Endersby opened his shop in Sleaford Street in 1884. When he retired, round about 1910, he passed the business on to Mrs William Osborn. Mrs Osborn sold practically everything too. The shop was also a post office, and the Victorian letter box in the wall outside is believed to be one of the oldest in Cambridge. It is also, in the expert opinion of Mr M.J. Towler of Haslingfield, extremely rare, there being fewer than 30 Victorian examples of the Ludlow type (which this is) still in use.

When Bob and Edna Wingrove took over the shop 32 years ago, it was a greengrocer's run by Harry Osborn. "Then it sold vegetables, vinegar and a few tins of peas," said Mrs Wingrove. She and her husband, who own nos. 3, 5 and 7 Ainsworth Street, which are shortly to be modernised under a welcome scheme for the area, are the focal point for the village-like community of Sleaford Street and some of the streets nearby. Some of the young families who have moved into the area tell you that "Edna will know", and during my researches I found that most roads led to Edna, or from her.

Sleaford Street is now a community of young and old. One of the oldest inhabitants is Mrs Hilda Sells, who has lived at no. 5 in a row of houses called Memorial Buildings since before she was married. "I was born at 81 Sturton Street in 1908. That house has now been pulled down. We later moved to 53 Sturton Street next to the school that was there. My father and mother were the school caretakers, and that is where I went to school. I remember when they used to drive the cattle up the street. Our governors used to put a blackboard at the door to stop the cows getting into the school." Mrs Sells' house in Sleaford Street is built on the site of a former orchard and she can remember the field, and the donkey in it, that was once at the bottom of York Terrace – that is where the oil tankers squeeze their way through.

For many people Sleaford Street is synonymous with the Co-op dairy, which has been at the end of the street by the railway siding for 25 years. It was opened on 15 October 1927 by Alderman J.E. Purvis, a member of the Public Health Committee and a Fellow of Corpus Christi College. The dairy got off to a good start retailing 400 gallons a day. Two years later extensions were made, and the abattoir was added. The milk was delivered by horse-drawn floats. Mr Donald Nelson, who joined the Co-op in 1927 and retired after 50 years' service, remembers the horses and ponies that drew the floats. "All the horses were stabled in Sturton Street. They were washed down every night. There was a big harness room and all the horses had their names up. The dairymen wore caps and livery."

They are all newcomers over in Rivar Place, where in recent years the houses on the west side, which were reprieved from demolition – those on the east side came down – have been attractively renovated and done up. The result is a quiet little mews, a row of whitewashed cottages with attractive number plates gleaming in the sun. Several of them are now the homes of doctors and nurses, who welcome the proximity to Mill Road.

16 York Street

19–26 January 1984

Home to generations of railway workers, York Street in Sturton Town was one of those streets developed by Joseph Sturton on what was formerly the Panton estate. Just outside the notorious slum area of Staffordshire Street and New Street, York Street was originally intended by Sturton to be an industrial development. His first building venture had been Gwydir Street – a mixed commercial and residential street. He sought to repeat the successful formula in York Street, and advertised the site in the *Cambridge Chronicle* for industrial development. The whole area, as Sturton pointed out in his advertisement, was nearer the railway station than the centre of town.

York Street turned out to be a bit of both. All the

York Street in 1984 – the characteristic Cambridge terrace street with the characteristic skip

newcomers flooding into Cambridge to work on the railways – and there were four railways running into Cambridge then – needed homes. Although the first inhabitants in the first 18 houses, built there by 1874, were local artisans – brickmakers, shoemakers, a paperhanger, a plasterer, a baker, a grocer – by 1884, three years after the 1881 census return had shown that more than half the inhabitants of Romsey Town had been born outside Cambridge, obviously drawn there by the work on the railways, York Street was a railway township in itself. Coal porters, firemen, railway servants, railway porters and railway carmen had all settled there.

By 1895 York Street consisted of 149 houses. They formed a parallel row of terraced cottages whose exteriors have not changed much in the past hundred years.

The part of the street nearest to New Street was

The Bible Class of 1922 at St Columba's Mission, York Street

called Lower York Street. The three houses on the west side of Lower York Street, situated on a slight incline, were much taller than the other houses in the vicinity. That incline, down to the little tree-lined recreation ground, was called by local children "Dobbler's Hole".

By 1885 York Street had its own Mission Hall in Lower York Street, now the Cambridgeshire College of Further Education. It was taken over by the congregation of St Columba's Church some ten years later, as part of the movement to improve the condition of the poor by philanthropic and missionary work. This concern for the poor in town districts throughout the country emanated from the colleges of Cambridge and Oxford in the late 19th century. The York Street Mission had been established in 1885 by three women: Miss Mary Elizabeth Watts, Mrs Macnaughton Egerton Brownlow and Miss Clifton. P.M. O'Neill, in "St Columba's York Street Mission", says that the two sisters, Mrs Margaret Gibson and Mrs Agnes Lewis, who founded Westminster College in 1899, bought the York Street Mission for St Columba's Church in 1905. At the end of 1906 the premises of the Mission were transferred to the trustees of the congregation, who saw it as "proving of value in the spiritual interest not only of the district but also of the congregation".

Mrs Lewis and Mrs Gibson, whose home was at Castlebrae in Chesterton Lane, continued to take an interest in the Mission. "They would come down for the Sunday evening service in their chauffeur-driven car and would take the Women's Meeting on Friday afternoons. They would often talk about their travels and had a coloured relief map of the Holy Land hung in the women's room," writes Miss O'Neill. There were Girls' Bible Class outings along the river to Baitsbite Lock and back for tea at

Castlebrae. "During the week there would be some activity practically every night at the Mission from which it was hoped communicants would be drawn." There was a Boys' Brigade, a Band of Hope, run by Dr Alex Wood at the Mission. In 1908 it had a membership of 130. From these groups grew a Young Men's and Young Ladies' Bible Class on Sunday afternoons and a large Sunday School. Mrs Gertrude Thompson, of 76 York Street, who lived as a child in Lower York Street, her father being the custodian at Romsey Recreation Ground, remembers attending Sunday School at the Mission. Her book was marked with a purple star to show that she had attended.

One of the great strengths of the Mission in the 1920s was the Joint Bible Class and Club, which was started in 1923. It had a strong social side, with club meetings on Mondays and Fridays with games of badminton, football, cricket, billiards, lexicon and draughts. The club also had a canteen, which the girls ran. Members directed their own amateur dramatics and musical evenings. It was also a friendly sick club, members paying 2 shillings to start with and then sixpence a week into a fund from which they drew when they were ill. Miss O'Neill makes the point that the club taught its members how to save and how helpful co-operative efforts were. Members of the Joint Club taught in the Sunday School and helped to sustain the work of the Mission which was of such vital importance to the whole community.

When the employees of Pye Unicam tuck into their lunch in the Unicam canteen on the west side of York Street, they may be unaware that their dining room was formerly a school, whose playground is now a kitchen. From 1882 to 1903 the building was the St Matthew's Higher Grade Boys' School, which had opened originally in Sturton Street in 1878. From 1904 to 1931 it was St Matthew's Boys' School, before it amalgamated with Norfolk Street Girls' to become a junior mixed and infants' school in 1933.

The log book of St Matthew's Church of England Boys' School from April 1920 to August 1931 gives us some insight into social conditions and standards at the school. There are frequent references to "malt and oil" boys attending clinics, and diptheria was prevalent in the 1920s. On 2 September 1924, His Majesty's Inspector for schools Mr J.F. Leat arrived to inspect St Matthew's. His report, inscribed in the log book, records: "There is a healthy tone in the school, and the boys exhibit a creditable interest in their work, which is executed with accuracy and neatness. Noticeable features are the attention paid to clear enunciation and the carefully thought-out scheme of handiwork. The general condition of the school under the new head teacher shows definite improvement." St Matthew's School, like St Columba's Mission, played a crucial part in the community life of the York Street neighbourhood – particularly in those inter-war years.

The recreation ground between York Street and Sturton Street

Among the many children who attended Sunday School at the Mission was Derek Stubbings, who now lives in Chesterton. Mr Stubbings, who is keenly interested in local history, was born at 94 York Street, at his grandparents' home. He remembers York Street as "a working man's street with its own dignity and sense of purpose". It was a closely knit community in which young couples and newlyweds tended to live "round the corner" from their parents. Mr Stubbings' grandmother lived in York Street close to her mother in Ainsworth Street. Mr Stubbings and his parents were round in St Matthew's Street. There were no long journeys involved in a visit to Granny!

Work was more or less on the spot, too. Railway workers didn't have far to go. Derek Stubbings' grandfather, Frederick Biggs, worked round in East Road for Gentle, the carrier, who had a supply of horses and carts rather than vans and lorries. "My grandfather left Gentle's in 1937 and went to become caretaker of Mansfield Hall, a men's Bible Class run by Mr Mansfield, the director of the University Farm." Now a busy street with traffic filtering up and down on its way to the Beehive, York Street in the 1920s had no motor traffic at all. It was a street of horses and carts. The local hearse from Weyman's in adjacent Abbey Walk was horse-drawn, and locals remember Tommy Cleares, the dealer who lived at no. 102 in the twenties and thirties. A horse and cart were vital to his livelihood.

Retired railway worker Conrad John Thompson and his wife Gertrude at 76 York Street. The son of a bootmaker, Mr Thompson was born at no. 77 in 1904

Another essential feature of life in York Street in those earlier days was the allotments. Residents kept pigs and grew vegetables on the ten-pole allotments, where the Beehive is now. The allotments covered the expanse of land between the east side of York Street and Coldham's Lane, now Co-op territory. A lane ran between the backs of the houses and the allotments. It was called Rope Walk and is clearly marked on the 1886 Ordnance Survey map. There is an obvious connection between Rope Walk and Simper's Ropeworks in New Street.

There have been social changes in York Street in the last ten years. It is no longer exclusively a working man's street. Young professional couples – doctors, teachers, etc. – are buying the houses, which the shortage and the cost of housing in the City have put into the £20,000 price bracket (they were probably built for around £100 each in the 1880s!). Like Gwydir Street, York Street is becoming gentrified. No. 26, the home of David Smith, a softwear computer engineer at Pye Unicam, and his wife Joanna, cost £26,500 in October 1983. It had already been modernised – which meant that the two up and two down cottage had had a bathroom installed. It needs little effort of the imagination to visualise conditions for the large families which lived in these little houses in the early days.

17 Gwydir Street

1–8 April 1982

A forest in Wales and an extensive moat are not the most obvious associations which spring to mind when you consider Gwydir Street off Mill Road. That's taking the rural imagery a bit far, surely? But no, the street is named after Lord Gwydir, whose family estates of Gwydir in County Caernarvon included the Gwydir Forest, near Ruthin. His wife, born Barbara Bertie in 1761, was the granddaughter of Thomas Panton, George II's chief equerry, who owned the open fields of Barnwell on which Gwydir Street was developed (see Abbey Road). The estate passed to Lady Gwydir and her son, who sold much of it to the Rev. Dr James Geldart in 1809. His family tried unsuccessfully in 1847 to auction off as building plots part of what is now the Mill Road end of Gwydir Street. The moat shows up on the sale catalogue of 1847 as two joined-up moated enclosures on land which is now about half-way down this long street.

In the late 1860s Joseph Sturton, the wholesale chemist in Fitzroy Street (see Sturton Street), bought a slab of land from the Geldarts and laid out Gwydir Street. Development started in the stretch between Norfolk Street and the corner of Hooper Street where the street is today blocked by bollards. Sturton chopped the land up into 16 ft-frontage blocks and these did extraordinarily well, being snapped up by prospective builders. The development from Hooper Street to Mill Road came rather later and some of these are bigger houses. Most of Gwydir Street belongs to the development of Sturton Town in the 1870s. By then a scheme to run a railway line from the station round the back of the cemetery to another station in Clarendon Street had finally been knocked on the head by Emmanuel and Christ's Colleges, and it became possible for builders to consider speculative development towards Mill Road. (Clarendon Street was one of many proposed railway terminii in Cambridge; the colleges vetoed it once they realised the station would need a goods yard as well.)

Gwydir Street corresponds to part of Eglantyne Jebb's description of the side streets off Mill Road in her *Cambridge: A Brief Study in Social Questions*, published in 1906: "On each side at right angles branch off little streets of small houses, some presenting the giddy monotony of a long succession of bay windows with here and there an attempt at ornament, a row of holes pierced in the parapet above the bay, or even a miniature Corinthian column dividing its front lights; other streets without bays, more severe and of equal uniformity, terminating occasionally in a general shop at the street corner."

By 1874, there were about 120 houses in Gwydir Street, only about one third of which were numbered. There were five pubs – the Brewer's Arms, the Dewdrop, the Gwydir Arms, the Alexandra Arms, and the Prince of Wales on the corner of Norfolk Street. A forerunner to Dale's Brewery (though possibly not on the same site) was Pilson and Newman's Brewery. The Gwydir Brewery is listed in the 1878 street directory. Railway workers – engine cleaners, engine drivers, guards and railway servants – and skilled artisans, such as masons, bricklayers, carvers, carpenters and foundrymen were among the first inhabitants. The Pamphilon Brothers, a firm of joiners, builders and undertakers, were established half-way down on the west side of the street. The Pamphilons were still there at the outbreak of the second world war. Gwydir Street in 1874 had its own resident policeman, Detective PC Edward Kirbyshire. There were several tailors, a marine store dealer by the name of Elijah Odell and several bootmakers. John Reynolds was the one harness maker and Mrs Spillman the only laundress listed. Mrs Spillman's great-granddaughter, Betty Sanderson of Cottenham, recalls being told by her grandfather "how he used to take the washing back and forth to the colleges for his mother – he would be about 12 years old then". It is likely that several women in the street took in washing. The census for 1881, which includes pages and pages on Gwydir Street but with all the packed houses unnumbered, records under the heading of occupation that one Eleanor Chapman, a widow of 36, "keeps a mangle". A mangle in those days was a labour-saving device equivalent to the deep-freeze today. Mrs Chapman would have been a respected lady – the local Mrs Tiggy-winkle!

By 1901, Gwydir Street was all there, a street of about 200 modest little terrace houses with equally modest rents, but the rents of the houses on the east side of the street were more expensive than of those on the west. Eglantyne Jebb worked out that the east side of Gwydir Street contained houses with rentals over £8 and not more than £15 per annum. The west side of the street and the workhouse towards the top contained houses with rentals of not more than £8 per annum. It was a street of poor families.

Social life was in full swing in the Beaconsfield Conservative Club by the turn of the century. Founded in 1884, the club was the Conservatives' reply to Sturton's political club for the Liberals built on Mill Road, which later became Sturton Town Hall. The Beaconsfield, named after Disraeli (who became the Earl of Beaconsfield), is now the venue for league darts matches and discos and the façade is crumbling, but in its heyday it was a great place. Shilling hops were held three times a week and the band made 7s 6d a night, according to Mr Ernest Cole of Ainsworth Street. Fiery political speeches were heard there. When in the spring of 1890 the Beaconsfield needed to raise funds to pay for urgent alterations, additions and improvements to the premises, they put on a "Fancy Fete and Bazaar" in the Corn Exchange. The bazaar was opened by the Duchess of Abercorn and the entertainment was wonderfully exotic. A jungle exhibition supplied from the collection of the Hon. Walter Lionel Rothschild included a group of silver-tipped grisly bears playing, and plumed birds of paradise. A French ventriloquist called Jean de Zello put on a "celebrated scene" and introduced his "Merry Wooden-headed Family". Admission to this spectacle was sixpence. You also paid to watch a marvellous "Japanese Juggling Performance", according to the programme in the Cambridgeshire Collection.

By the turn of the century, there were more shopkeepers and tradesmen in Gwydir Street than in the 1870s. Three butchers, two greengrocers, two fishmongers, two grocers and a baker, John Harwood, are listed in the street directory for 1901. Mrs Sarah Fergusson ran a second-hand clothes shop from her home at no. 47, while H. Rogers made baskets at no. 97. Up on the west side, just off Mill Road, lived the custodian of Parker's Piece, Alfred Nunn. Mr Nunn's house, no. 183, stood next to some stables, later the site of Dale's Brewery, which moved from behind the British Queen at Histon Road to Gwydir Street in the early years of this century. It was founded by Mr Frederick Dale in the 1890s, at which time there were no fewer than 22 breweries in Cambridge. For many years Dale's Brewery building,

Gwydir Street today, with the controversial bollards which put an end to through traffic

Dale's Brewery delivery van in the 1920s, replacing the old horse-drawn drays

now in a desecrated state and with an uncertain future, was marked by a 7-ft high copper cup representing the gold cup won by Dale's for the best beer at the Brewers' International Exhibition in 1911. It was said that members of the Cambridge boat race crew trained on Dale's beer. The tradition was carried on by the Whitbread Company which took over Dale's Brewery as a distribution depot. Gothic House, no. 184, was occupied in 1901 by George G. Walter, the relieving officer and inspector under the Infant Life Protection Act, District no. 3. He was obviously the local "nob".

By the early 1920s, Gwydir Street was home to at least 14 carpenters and as many plasterers and decorators. It had a haycutter too, J.W. Newman, who lived at no. 111. Sydney Pratt, the magical entertainer who died recently, set off for the first world war from his home at no. 155. The high spot of the late 1920s in Gwydir Street was the opening of the City of Cambridge Public Baths in February 1927 for the use of cleanly citizens without baths. It replaced the doctor's house at the junction of Gwydir Street and Mill Road. In the late 1930s, the baths were open from Mondays to Fridays from 10 a.m. to 1 p.m. and from 2 p.m. to 8 p.m., and on Saturdays from 10 a.m. to 8 p.m. The charge then was fourpence per bath. The price went up to one shilling some years later. In 1978 the Bath House

was saved from demolition by the St Matthew's Neighbourhood Association and Friends of the Earth. They formed the Bath House Trust to convert it into a neighbourhood community centre with low-rent office accommodation for voluntary and community groups in the City. The building, now warm and comfortable, is completely self-supporting and is the focus of a number of community activities; and a Saturday morning market operates from the Bath House Garden.

As I cycled out one fine spring morning into Gwydir Street, I overhead this social snippet: "I've got a deadline on a chapter of my thesis next week." Nowadays, street natter down there is frequently rather esoteric. It is often about country matters too, because this is a patch of Cambridge where the professional middle class have shown themselves in the past decade to be dab hands at animal husbandry, rearing chickens, bees and sometimes goats in their long back gardens. One goat breeder with a kid that showed no interest in being weaned from a bottle even got down on his hands and knees and munched grass in a vain attempt to show this truculent animal what real feeding was all about.

There is a precedent for animals and wild life in Gwydir Street. At one time the elephants coming to perform in the circuses on Midsummer Common were "billeted" in the stables at the back of the old Brewer's Arms, while a chimney sweep called Sanderson kept an enormous parrot which used to swear for five minutes on a Sunday without using the

same word twice. Cows were driven down Gwydir Street on a Monday afternoon on their way from the cattle market to the two slaughteryards in Gwydir Street. The pigs and sheep came by truck. One of these yards stood opposite the Beaconsfield Club.

Mrs Joyce Pring, who has lived at 172 Gwydir Street for 51 years and was born at no. 97 in 1920, can remember the car-park next to the Bath House being an orchard with cottages and stables. She recalls the time when the centre of Cambridge was flooded: "The water ran down Bridge Street. I can remember a layer of water on the floor at Sainsburys, that's when it was up near Woolworths." Mrs Pring was one of those people who bought her first dress at Marks and Spencer for 1s 11d. Her father was a carpenter, and her mother an upholstress who made all the covers for the furniture in King's College Hostel when it was first opened in Peas Hill.

Joyce Pring can remember the house nearly opposite her being built – no. 165, belonging to Sam and Pat Motherwell. This highly individual looking residence formerly belonged to John Kent, a slater and tiler who lived next door at Bahia Cottage, no. 167, later the home of Herbert Finbow, whose father William Robert Finbow started his removal business at no. 152 in 1910 with three horses, two vans, a hansom cab and a small landau. On retirement in 1936, Mr Kent built himself a house on the site of his slater's yard, the front of which had been used as an advertising hoarding. As Pat Motherwell relates, "Mr Kent left a lot of his slates behind at the bottom of the garden – the patio in front of the house is composed of cast-off slate slabs." The Motherwells moved into their home from 160 Gwydir Stret, effecting the art of the house-hop, which seems to be quite common practice in this big street. You hang on until your dream residence sports a "For Sale" sign (offers over £30,000 for one painted-up house in the street this week), or else you buy the house next door and make two into one. The attraction of the houses on the east side is their gardens. Very long. Some at the Mill Road end back onto the maternity hospital, others, further down, onto the cemetery, where local joggers take their exercise, and where 77 new trees have recently been planted. You can take a bit of a country ramble in the Motherwells' garden, past the garden seat, down through the lawn and flower garden, to the kitchen garden and the chickens. Peek over the hedge and see one of Gwydir Street's two composers, Larif Freedman, sitting in his garden at work. Over at no.

The Mill Road end of Gwydir Street with Dale's Brewery and the Collectors' Market on the left

160 lives John Hopkins, the other well-known young composer.

First prize for the biggest garden in Gwydir Street must go to the Sanders family, who live at no. 145. It used to be the workhouse garden, and was acquired by the Sanders when plans for developing the maternity hospital on the land were dropped in the early 1970s. It is a real "secret garden" with an old pump, a mature walnut tree which neighbours remember being planted, and the original winding paths along which the inmates of the workhouse would have taken compulsory exercise. Shin up the trees at the end of the garden and you'll give a fright to patients in the ante-natal ward. The Sanders house had not changed hands since it was built, said Mary Sanders, a chemistry teacher, whose husband David is a systems analyst. It had belonged to a family of missionaries called Lambert. When the Sanders moved in, they found a lot of antlers in the attic. Trophies from African tours of duty?

What other street anywhere in the world, let alone Cambridge, contains not only two composers but two, yes two, harpsichord makers. For the past nine and a half years, Trevor Beckerleg has been making two or three harpsichords a year in his workshop at the back of what used to be Mill's Grocery. Further down, in Upper Gwydir Street, nearly opposite the Norfolk Street Post Office, which serves a key social function, is Mark Stevenson. He makes harpsichords in what used to be the old Salvation Army schoolroom. Still on the musical theme, there's Daniel Bangham, who lives at no. 121. He makes copies of clarinets and repairs wind instruments in his workshop in Felton Street. The applied arts are also well represented in the street. In fact, the keeper of the Applied Arts Department at the Fitzwilliam Museum, Robin Crichton, lives there with his wife, who is a child psychologist. Warwick "Wocky" Hutton, the art lecturer at CCAT, who is a glass engraver and book illustrator, has recently moved from Warkworth Street to join the clans of Tech lecturers in Gwydir Street. He and his family own no. 29, once the milk shop belonging to Biggs' Dairy. Frederick Charles Biggs used to live there. In the 1920s it was a fruiterer's and florist's, run by Harry Miller. Local people still remember the milk shop. "When I pulled up the blind in the front window," said Lizzie Hutton, "some old people walking past said 'there's the milk shop'."

Art teacher Ron Nix lives at no. 12, built in 1870, one of the few detached houses in the street. (It is the Nixes' second move in Gwydir Street.) Fring House, obviously *the* house in that part of the street, has been home over the years to carpenters (it was probably built by one), a surgeon (1884–7), a col-

The Bath House at the corner of Gwydir Street and Mill Road

lege baker, a boot salesman, the headmistress Miss Thompson (1931–4), and a chemist's assistant, from whom the Nixes bought the house in 1974. Ron Nix and his wife Min are both involved in the St Matthew's Neighbourhood Association, which has done all those good things at the Bath House.

Another popular local activist is Roy Hammans at 71 Gwydir Street. He is a photographer with the University and is the man to see if you want to get in on the Dark Room at the Bath House. He was able to tell me last week that the general feeling among residents on the issue of the moment is that a centre for the unemployed in what used to be Dale's Brewery would be acceptable, provided the control on noise was very strict. Roy Hammans' wife Carol is secretary of the local cat collective started by Miss Joan Court in Sturton Street. Considered a joke when it was set up, it has proved successful in re-uniting lost cats with their distraught owners. The cat collective has taken the headache out of holiday planning. Pussy will be fed! The Hammans have made a pretty home out of their modest Gwydir Street house. They enjoy a panoramic view of the cemetery from their balcony on the first floor.

Gwydir Street has taken in refugees from the Kite. Anthony Jones has opened "Period Piece" opposite Hooper Street and helps new inhabitants in the area furnish their homes. Ladies from Cavendish Road were acquiring brass door knobs when I was there. I liked the slipper chamber pot full of gorgeous coloured marbles. The Collectors' Market has found sanctuary up at the Mill Road end of Gwydir Street, after having to leave Fitzroy Street. Another new centre of enterprise is no. 25 – the "old Pye building". This is being adapted to accommodate a number of small businesses, and at present it houses the editorial and translation agency First Edition, an entertainment agency, a typesetter, an author, a leather worker, a contact lens manufac-

Harpsichord maker Trevor Beckerleg in his workshop

turer, a printer and a drama wardrobe – and there are several units still to be filled.

So they come; and go. Among those who have recently moved out of the street is Robert Crabtree, the Tech lecturer, who used to keep chickens. He is said to have gone to Australia to start a vineyard.

Houses don't remain empty for long in Gwydir Street, the Camden Town of Cambridge. It is a popular place to live and its residents include the niece of the Duke of Devonshire. All rather a far cry from the days when you bought your pint of paraffin from Brown's hardware shop at no. 64, or your sweets from the little shop across the road. The shops have gone, and the intelligentsia have moved in.

18 Norfolk Street

26 March 1981

Norfolk Street is part of Cambridge's own cheery East End. Knocked about in recent years and subsequently redeveloped, it is still a real community street where you might well expect to die in the house where you had been born some 80 years before. (Longevity appears to be a notable attribute of the area.)

Cockney-type jokes about the proximity of the cemetery are liable to surface in conversations about the street. A robustness of spirit in the face of adversity characterises the local residents, and there is not too much lamenting the "good old days", probably because they weren't all that good for the

Flo Harben, one of the oldest residents in Norfolk Street

working man. Originally it was a street of artisan dwellings, built on what had been open fields. The go-ahead, as it were, for the building of Norfolk Street, followed the final abandonment in the 1860s of the plan to run a railway line round from the station to another station in Clarendon Street.

By 1874 Norfolk Street was there, and its inhabitants included a blacksmith, a shoemaker, a cellarman, a grocer's foreman, a coal agent, a wheelwright, a carpenter and dairyman, a maltster, a butcher, a tailor and a bootmaker. In adjacent Norfolk Terrace lived a nurse, several tailors, a bricklayer, a millwright, an engine driver at Foster's Mill down by the Mill Pond, a college cook, a college laundress and a college servant, together with a boatman, a fencing master and a bootmaker. A tennis marker and a strawbonnet and hat maker were among the residents in Norfolk Buildings, according to the street directory for 1874.

Miss Enid Porter, the late curator of the Cambridge Folk Museum, recalled that her grandmother was born at 13 Norfolk Street, now part of the premises of A.H. Frost Ltd, the drapers. Born Miss Barrett, Miss Porter's grandmother became Mrs Scott when she married. She must have been one of the first residents of the street. Folk memory recalls a workhouse in nearby Staffordshire Street, a coalyard on what used to be the site of the old St Matthew's School in Norfolk Street (now a piece of waste ground by the paper shop), and a malting house over the street in what is now the Alex Wood Hall, the headquarters of the Cambridge Labour Party. It doesn't need a trained eye to spot those malting house chimneys – just take a walk down Norfolk Terrace. The malting house became a knitting factory before it became the Labour Party HQ in 1927. It cost £1,000 to buy and £1,500 to alter.

At one time Norfolk Street was well endowed with pubs. There was the Old Norfolk (on the side of the street that was demolished), the Royal Engineers, the Swan (sometimes called the White Swan or the Old Swan), the Prince of Wales and, round in Staffordshire Street, the Man in the Moon, later rebuilt as the Man on the Moon in the new Norfolk Street shopping precinct – it was given its

Mr and Mrs G. B. Taylor outside their award-winning fish and chip shop at 61 Norfolk Street

new name after Neil Armstrong had done his stuff up in space. The Swan and the Prince of Wales are now both private houses. When the removal men were moving the Printz-Pahlsons (they are Swedish) into the Swan at 77 Norfolk Street, they told Mrs Ulla Printz-Pahlson that it had been a very rough tough pub, and that "the Law had been down there every night". In the spacious, book-lined drawing room with a vase of mimosa on the table, it requires an effort of one's imagination to visualise "goings on" in the lounge bar. At the back of the house is a south-facing patio where a fertile vine yields 100 pounds of grapes a year. That sounds more like it!

One of the oldest residents in the area is Mrs Florence Harben, who lives at 39 Norfolk Terrace. Born in 1892 at 54 Norfolk Street, she talks cheerfully about the old days. "My father was a hairdresser at the top of Norfolk Street. He brought up 12 children – six lovely girls and six lovely boys – on a penny shave and twopenny haircut." Mrs Harben, whose husband was a Norfolk Street butcher, told me that "We used to have a garden down Staffordshire Street where we used to kill our pigs." She is one of those local people for whom the cemetery is an important part of the landscape. She says: "If I get down-hearted I go to the bottom of my garden and say: 'Bless your hearts, you are better off than what we are.' I was married in St Matthew's Church and I want to be there when I die," she said with a smile.

Mr Terrence "Terry" Whitehead has lived in Norfolk Street for 71 years. Until he retired six years ago, he used to run a greengrocery business at no. 45. The shop was in the front room, which is now Mr Whitehead's living room. His father, Mr Frank Whitehead, started the business there. Norfolk Street has evolved as a street of shopkeepers, providing a High Street type of service which would be the envy of a more residential area. Contemporary memory recalls the row of shops which lined the north side of the road, demolished some 20 years ago for the council flats development. Mr Whitehead remembers Goodes, the sweetshop across the road. "Next to Goodes there was a general store and a little shop which sold whelks. Townsend's the cycle shop, now over in Burleigh Street, was opposite us, together with Mason's the chemist, which also moved to Burleigh Street. That was a good many years ago." Everyone remembers the Co-op on the corner of St Matthew's and Norfolk Streets. Mr Whitehead can go further back than that. He recalls the dairy in Blossom Street. "They used to take the cows to the common." Next door to Mr Whitehead lived the two Maltby brothers. "They were robemakers who made gowns for the undergraduates." The famous award-winning fish and chip shop run by Mr and Mrs G.B. Taylor at 61 Norfolk Street used to be the curate's house, says the Rev. S. Sims, vicar of St Matthew's Church. "That was some 50 to 60 years ago." Mr Taylor's parents started the fish shop when they came to Norfolk Street in 1935.

F.T. Unwin, in his book *Pimbo and Jenny in Old Cambridge*, describes in detail the old Norfolk Street shop of Mr Haynes, which used to stand on the corner of St Matthew's Street. "Mr Haynes was affectionately known as Hummer Haynes, as throughout his entire serving procedure, he would be intently humming a current song theme. High on the shelves were stocked huge bins with the name of its contents printed in bold letters: Sugar, Tea, Rice, Sago, Tapioca, Beans, Coffee. Every item of grocery was kept in one of these bins. Subsequently, Hummer would weigh each request meticulously into a blue paper, which he would roll expertly into a bag. Butter was patted into submission, cheese wired into sizeable portions, bacon sliced, and every conceivable item had to be weighed and packed by the master grocer. A housewife ordering a complete week's groceries would have to wait as Hummer,

Colin Walsh, one of the directors of Book Production Consultants, which moved into Norfolk Street in 1983. The firm handles the production of hundreds of books each year, including Down Your Street

being the only server in the shop, painstakingly 'got up' her order. With the advent of quicker serving facilities introduced into other shops, Mr Haynes gradually lost his customers – but housewives swore that his humming grew more intent."

Mr Richard Frost, together with his brother Peter, of Frosts the drapers, recalls that their father, a grocer and draper in Haverhill before he came to Cambridge to found the Norfolk Street business, viewed the advent of the supermarket with deep misgiving. "When the International Stores came to Haverhill, father said, 'when supermarkets come here then it is time to get out'. When he was in business in Haverhill, he used to come into Cambridge once a week. He would park his Ford on the Cattle Market because there was too much traffic for him to get into Eaden Lilley's," said Mr Richard, as he is known by his staff. And what are the changes in the clothing business that Mr Richard is most aware of? "Millinery is the big change. It used to be Easter bonnets, but now separates and jeans have taken over." In the old days, Frosts used to sell "a lot of maids' clothes".

During the last war, Frosts' cellar was one of the air raid shelters for the locality. Two other air raid

shelters were in Gas Lane, as Miss Iris Franklin, the former headmistress of St Matthew's Infant School, told me. "I did the billeting for the evacuees during the war," she said. "We used to go after school to what is now the Young Street College to make gas masks. We fitted both the children and the local elderly people with gas masks in the school. It was reassuring for the old people to come to us in the school." Miss Franklin, who lives at 3 Mackenzie Road, went to St Matthew's in 1935 and became headmistress of the Infant School in 1946. She retired in 1975. A new section of St Matthew's School is currently being built in Caroline Place, parallel to Norfolk Street. During the war, with the evacuee children from three London schools to be fitted into the school, the building that in recent years has been St Matthew's Church Hall was used as part of St Matthew's School. It had been built as a school in 1871; the separate girls' and boys' entrances are still identified over the doors. There is now a planning application pinned to the door for a change of use "from church hall to light industrial use".

Among Miss Franklin's former pupils were Roy Townsend and the sons of Ada Warwick. Mrs Warwick ran a second-hand shop at 3 Norfolk Street and was one of the great Norfolk Street characters. The building firm of Johnson and Bailey which used to be in Norfolk Street was a great tradition in the area. Miss Franklin recalls that they did quite a lot of work for the school. Perhaps St Matthew's School's most famous old boy was the English cricketer, Jack Hobbs (see Sleaford Street). Mr Frank Wilson, the saddler and harness maker at no. 11, has been in business there about 33 years. He took the business over from Mr Octavius Ruse, who was also a saddler. A skilled craftsman, he contributes to the reputation of Norfolk Street as a street where it must be possible to find just about anything you want. Among the other well-established shop-keepers are Mr R.B. Speechley, the butcher, and Bridgemans, the bakers, which used to be Taylors of Staffordshire Street. The Bridgeman brothers, Richard and Walter, start their day at 3.30 a.m. when they get up to make the bread. They have been in business for 34 years.

Among the newcomers to the street are Mike and Jill Smith, who run the large antique shop at 5–7 Norfolk Street. It used to be Freemans, the furniture store. Mr Richard Frost tells how Freemans used to do a house removal for 12s 6d for a full day's work. The Smiths' speciality is restoring furniture. They have a French polisher, an upholsterer and a pine stripper all working for them. Mike Smith presents the Yorkshire television programme, "As Good As New", which is about restoring antiques. Among the many treasures for sale in their shop, the Smiths have a selection of old toys, many of which are now collectors' items. I was intrigued to see a childhood friend, Muffin the Mule, of TV fame, for sale at £12.

Gordon Ison at 9 Norfolk Street is a refugee from James Street. He misses not being able to stand his second-hand items and tools out in front of the shop as he used to in James Street. He would like to get back there where trade was better. "People don't like crossing the main road, East Road, to get here." He is in favour of an underpass from Burleigh Street, which formerly, they say, was the shopping Mecca for the people from the Norfolk Street–Gwydir Street area. Changes there have been in Norfolk Street – an influx of students and younger people who have bought houses there – but the real character of the street hasn't changed. It is still a community with a jolly decent selection of shops, the old ones being supplemented by, among others, a greengrocer, a hairdresser, a restaurant and a grocer in the new precinct.

19 Willis Road

22 September 1983

Willis Road, better known now as "Silicon Alley", is an unpretentious street of late Victorian houses built on land belonging to Caius College just past the G.P.O. sorting office off Mill Road. It use to be one of those streets of which people would say, "Yes, near the Tech, but which one?" But since Sir Clive Sinclair established one of the powerhouses of British industry – Sinclair Research Ltd – in a space age bubble of a building on the site of C. Barker's mineral water bottling plant, at the end of Willis Road behind the Cambridgeshire College of Arts and Technology, the street has become rather well known. It was the subject of a full page advertisement in a Sunday newspaper two weeks ago. Since then, the name "Silicon Alley" – a good copywriter's slogan – has rather stuck. The site of Sinclair Research retains one direct link with the past, according to that advertisement. The old mineral water well, whether or not it was therapeutic, has one valuable characteristic: it maintains a constant temperature of 128°F, all the year round. Sinclair has incorporated it into a heating system for the building which helps reduce energy costs.

Sir Clive is not the only entrepreneur to have pitched camp, as it were, in Willis Road; Mr C. Barker, the mineral water bottler, was a worthy predecessor who set up in business in the closing years of Queen Victoria's reign. And before Sir Clive moved in the factory was occupied for 16 years by the office equipment and stationery suppliers John Moore and Beeson (now at the University Printing House). Another equally important entrepreneur lived in Willis Road – no. 12 – when the houses were first built in the 1890s. He was William Farrow Taylor, founder of the *Cambridge News*.

"It was no elaborate study of the potential market but an act of faith which determined the birth of the *Cambridge News*," writes Mr A.J.H. Durham, managing director of Cambridge Newspapers Ltd, in an unpublished account of the history of the *Cambridge News*. "In 1888 William Farrow Taylor, a Victorian character of strength and independence, came to Cambridge from Bury St Edmunds, and putting his trust in his own business instinct and in the help of a few friends founded the first evening newspaper to be published in the City. It took courage. The population then stood at no more than 36,000, and although a flourishing community sustained by the University and a prosperous agriculture, commercial activity showed few signs of growth."

The early years of the *Cambridge Daily News*, as it was then known, were not without struggle, and it might not have survived to record even the turn of the century, had it not been for the support of its companion, the *Cambridge Weekly News*, which was founded at the same time and quickly achieved popularity, despite fierce opposition. To beat off the competition, the *Daily News* adopted a strict economy. For instance, a horse and trap toured the City on a Friday to collect payment for advertising, so that the wages could be paid the following day. The horse, apparently, came to know the route without prompting, and even stopped unbidden at the pubs favoured by its driver. It was through the abilities of the founder, and later his third son, "a man cast in a similar mould", according to Mr Durham, that the *Weekly News* "was able to obtain both predominance and ancestry by successively engulfing its competitors".

By 1901 William Farrow Taylor had moved across Parker's Piece to Camden House in Park Terrace, just around the corner from the *News* in St Andrew's Street. His near neighbours in Willis Road in those early days, when many houses were still being built, were John Iliffe, the headmaster of Paradise Street Higher Grade School (quite a coincidence, because the *News* was acquired in 1959 by Lord Iliffe and later his son), and the Rev. George Nickson, a tutor at Ridley Hall. John Stacy Youngman, an accountant with offices in Downing Street, lived at no. 14. Willis Road continued to be inhabited by teachers and clerics. Among them in 1901 were the assistant master at the Perse, the Rev. E. Creswell Gee; he was also the assistant curate at All Saints. His neighbour was the Rev. Charles Howard, curate-in-charge at St Philip's Church. By

OPPOSITE: *The Sinclair Research building in Willis Road*

Looking up Willis Road to Mill Road

1911 the headmaster of St Philip's Boys' School, Arthur Meakin, had moved to no. 7 and Miss G. Blair, headmistress of the Higher Grade Girls' School, and Miss A.P.T. Iliffe, headmistress of St Barnabas' Girls' School, were living at no. 11.

The newspaper element returned in 1931–2, when no. 14 was the home of C.T. Wilkins, the managing director of the *Cambridge Chronicle*. Councillor Justin Kenney lived at no. 8. Next door at no. 6 was John Cecil Evered, the dental surgeon; his widow, Constance Knott-Craig, still lives in the house with their son Laurence. Mrs Knott-Craig recalls the days when the houses were inhabited by families and private residents, whereas now most of them are divided into flats. Mr Evered, who works for Pye, remembers that the Salvation Army regu-larly used to play at the Mill Road end of Willis Road every Sunday night.

At the outbreak of the second world war, the Norfolk Regiment was billeted in houses in Willis Road, and after Dunkirk, Scottish soldiers were similarly housed. During the war a stick of bombs dropped close by, near Fenner's Cricket Ground. Many people will remember the Nevinson sisters, who lived at 10 Willis Road for many years; Miss Bridget Nevinson, who died a year or so ago, was a staunch supporter of St Botolph's Church in Trump-ington Street. They were related to the Victorian artist of the same name. Willis Road's modern claim to fame, Sir Clive Sinclair's business, has generated a lot of local interest. Residents are proud of "their" innovator and all he has done to put Cambridge on the new technology map.

20 East Road

31 May–28 June 1984

With the County Council's proposals for its widening, East Road has become the most contentious highway in Cambridge. By any historical reckoning, it is entirely inappropriate that what was once a medieval thoroughfare should become a mini autobahn. There are allusions to it in the early rent rolls called the Barnwell terriers, which were based on the Priory Fields Books of the early 14th century. These terriers, which divided the open medieval East Field into six parcels, each made up of a different number of strips called sellions, refer to East Road as "the old Mill Way". Four hundred years later we find it with a new name. In the 1811 enclosure award East Road is marked as Gravel Pit Road. There are frequent references to gravel pits in the Barnwell terriers, particularly in the area

The Robert Moden oil, paint, varnish and general stores at 81 East Road near the junction with New Street in the early 1900s

around what later became Norfolk Street. And there are those who can still recall the gravel pits behind the cottages that stood on East Road until 1962 opposite Coulsons, the builders.

From medieval times until the Enclosure Act of 1806–7 Gravel Pit Road was the boundary between two of the six Barnwell fields, Clayangles (85 acres of land in the area between Jesus College, Midsummer Common, Parker Street, Parkside, East Road and Newmarket Road) and Bradmore or Bradmere, which was much bigger. Bradmore field, which has given its name to the little street beside the Zion Chapel where today CCAT students park their motorbikes, covered 261 acres between Newmarket Road, East Road and Mill Road to the edge of Hinton Moor, a large tract of marshy land which extended from Hills Road to Coldham's Common. Nor far from Gravel Pit Road on wet land near the future site of the Mill Road Cemetery was an osier bed. Just to the south a footpath ran across the fields

Before Elizabeth Way – a view of the junction of East Road and Newmarket Road in 1962

linking Mill Road, where lots of barley was grown on the land opposite the windmill which gave its name to Mill Road, to New Street, where building began soon after enclosure. Leonard Amey of Cherry Hinton Road, author of an article on the history of Barnwell Fields, thinks that the mill which gave East Road its earlier name of "the old Mill Way" was on the highest part of East Road.

Building didn't start on East Road or on the land to either side of it until after enclosure, but then it got going at a rate, particularly at the top and near the junction with Newmarket Road, formerly Barnwell Street, where there was quite a jigsaw of enclosure allotments. Leonard Amey refers to this dense housing as "the Barnwell congestion", which shows up clearly on R.G. Baker's map of 1830. He writes: "Behind the respectable terraces of Maid's Causeway the small cottages have already been packed in. Even more are going up in the area bounded by Sun Street, Wellington Street, Nelson Street and East Road, where 13 small allotments have been made behind existing houses. More low-grade development took place on land that was still Panton's at enclosure [see Abbey Road], round Abbey Street, New Street and Staffordshire Street, as well as in courts and yards off Newmarket Road itself. The later rate books for the parish of St Andrew the Less

estimate the rent of cottages in this area at no more than £2 10s a year. This low-grade housing finally extended into the old gravel pits off East Road, partly to accommodate construction workers on the railway."

But not all the East Road houses were small cottages. An advertisement in the *Cambridge Chronicle* for 9 June 1815 refers to a "pleasant new-erected house, Barnwell, to be sold by auction at the Angel Inn, Cambridge, on Tuesday the 20th day of June, 1815, at seven o'clock in the evening." The fulsome advertisement in Georgian estate agent's parlance describes the "handsome, new-erected house" as being "delightfully situated on the East Road leading from Regent street into Barnwell, containing two good parlours, with recess closets, light kitchen with dresser and sink, four very cheerful bed-rooms, and excellent cellaring. The House stands in a pleasant garden, protected from the road by neat green palisade fencing in which are a pair of large carriage gates, opening on to a circular gravel'd road to the House; attached to the premises is a pump of excellent water, and behind is a large piece of ground which will afford an abundant garden." Elliott Smith, the auctioneers, claimed that "the prospects from this delightful residence are beautiful, presenting to the eye in every direction a luxuriance which must gratify the most fascinating [fastidious?] taste." Nearly two months later, on 4 August 1815, Elliott Smith auctioned 12 building lots in East Road, "each in width 39 feet, and in depth 100 feet."

We hear again of property in East Road for sale in 1842 – part of the estate of the bankrupt miller James Nutter: two freehold brick and slate houses near the Blackbirds public house, one of which was a baker's shop with six rooms, a bake office and a 14-bushel oven (annual rent £15), and another "Brick-and-Slate Freehold House", 33 Broad Street, East Road. These were sold subject to an annuity of £71 per annum being paid to "a Female during her life, aged about Seventy-Eight, who has also her Life-Interest in the House No. 33, Broad street, and is to receive two chaldrons of good duck coals every year to be delivered at her residence." Another house in Broad Street, East Road, was also in the sale; this was occupied by William Driver, a baker who had an 11-bushel oven, "a neat paved yard, excellent Pump of water, Outbuildings etc.; together with an Entrance into South Street and East Road." His annual rent was £10.

By the 1850s East Road and adjacent streets and alleys in Barnwell had earned an East End reputation. Densely populated, with scores of public houses and beer retailers as well as brothels, it was a part of Cambridge which respectable people steered clear of, if a colourful feature entitled "The Dens and Traditions of Barnwell" in the *Cambridge Chronicle* of 8 January 1853 is anything to go by. "Barnwell," wrote the sensitive author, "improved as it has been during the past few years, is still the focus of villainy, the receptacle of dishonest spoil, the refuge of the petty thief and the full developed scoundrel. And we defy any mortal living to visit its dark entries, its tortuous windings, its many secret approaches from the country, its scores of segments, its trap-doors, and its zig-zag passages, or to note its sombre, wild, dilapidated, filthy leprous features, without being deeply impressed with the belief that it has been fashioned by the hand of crime to meet the direful requirements of criminals." The reader was invited to enter "some of these crime-stained abodes." He is told: "It is in the afternoon; you are on the East-road, and . . . you go into Crispin-passage. The abodes are cheerless, squalid; their occupants eye you with a restless, wistful glance, and then shun your sight; they are for the greater part idle, dissolute characters. The men are known to the police; the women live, and partly support their paramours, by perpetual dishonour." Old Gas Lane, where "all is poverty, and barren dreariness", is described as the "receptacle of all the physical dross of Cambridge".

Strong stuff indeed. "Union-row, commonly called 'Devil's-row', is another delightful retreat for the

Blacksmith and publican Joe Day (he and his family ran the Britannia public house) outside Donald MacKay's Engineering Works in East Road in the early 1900s

freebooter: it runs from Fitzroy street into East-road; it is a sort of sepulchral vault where morals are entombed, and infamy reigns without a rival." The population of Barnwell in those Victorian times was vast. The census return for 1851 contains pages and pages listing families packed into little cottages in Bradmore Street, Broad Street, School House Lane, Brewhouse Lane, Staffordshire Street and all the other alleys and yards making up the higgledy-piggledy back streets off East Road.

By the 1860s East Road itself was established as a street full of typical 19th-century artisan enterprises. Besides the numerous beer retailers there were marine store dealers, corn merchants, cabinet makers, butchers, grocers, saddlers, and a bone and manure works called R. and H. Walton. There was one pawnbroker, Mary Nash, at no. 182, in the stretch between Burleigh Street and Dover Street. For many of these working-class families income would have been supplemented by the wives working as laundresses.

One of the oldest firms in East Road is Coulsons,

the builders, who are celebrating their centenary this year. In 1884 at the age of 21, Herbert Charles Coulson, a carpenter, began his own business as a builder trading from premises in Burleigh Street. In 1889 he took a partner, William Lofts, and they traded as Coulson and Lofts from 158 East Road, with a town office at 37 St Andrew's Street. The 1886 street directory lists a Joseph Coulson, builder, at 171 East Road; Mrs Hilda Wilderspin of St Margaret's Road, Girton, writes to me that this was her uncle. "Joseph and Herbert were brothers and Joseph went off to America, I think through some quarrel." In the early days the firm did a lot of work in the south and east of England and was responsible for some speculative development in Willis Road and Harvey Goodwin Avenue – all part of Cambridge's Victorian building boom. They had a large joinery works in East Road which is still in existence, and a stonemason's works in Newmarket Road, which subsequently moved to its present site in East Road. When Herbert Coulson died in 1921 the firm became a private limited company, Coulson and Son Ltd, with W.G. James, who had joined in 1911, as managing director. After he died in 1962 the company continued under the direction of his sons, John Thomas and Robert James.

A wealth of minute detail about the early history of the firm came to light when Mr W.G. James tackled the contents of a long-forgotten deed box

Horse-drawn tram in East Road on Wednesday, 18 February 1914, the day of the last horse-drawn tram run in Cambridge. The tram is standing outside the depot with the horse facing towards Newmarket Road. The manager, Mr E. Thomas, is the man in the bowler hat and heavy coat standing underneath the "largest stocks in Eastern Counties" sign. Mr Willis, the horsekeeper, is wearing a heavy waistcoat and stands next to the man in a coat and cap on the right

just before his death. As well as information about income tax rates (only a halfpenny in the £ in 1911–12 and 1913) and about the firm's profitability – £631 in 1890, rising to £1,534 in 1903 and falling during the first world war to £218 in 1916 – he culled from the mass of old papers some social snippets which may awaken memories. There was a works outing to Great Yarmouth in July 1912. The 60 dinners cost 2s 6d each and eight gallons of lemonade were drunk at a cost of 2s per gallon. Christmas boxes that year were cigars and cigarettes from Fribourg and Freyer, at a charge of 10s 4d for 31 Cuba cigars, 2s 3d for 53 special Virginia cigarettes, and 11d for two ounces of pipe tobacoo. Another interesting archive refers to the purchase of 37 St Andrew's Street in May 1908 for £2,300, premises which the firm had been using as offices since 25 March 1901 at a yearly rental of £60. The sale notice prepared by Rutters, the auctioneers, says that the property was "formerly known as Michael House Grange and probably used as the Farm House for the land which is now Parker's Piece." W.G. James' notes say that "the farm also included 36 St Andrew's Street".

In the week when we commemorate the 40th anniversary of the D-Day landings in Normandy it is interesting to note that during the second world war Coulsons were mainly involved in defence contracts, including work at many East Anglian air fields, coastal fortifications and radar stations. Straight after the war, local authority housing was the priority. Coulsons have always had a large workforce. Back in 1901 they employed 260 men, according to an article in the *Cambridge Graphic* for 6 July 1901. "They have executed orders in various parts of the country including Ramsgate, Broadstairs, Chelmsford, Reading and many parts of London." Many of these jobs involved fitting up public houses for Ind Coope and Co. Ltd, noted Mr James. The article says that of the 260 men, "there are about 50 employed at the mill and workshop. There are

A plate showing the Britannia Works of Donald MacKay in 1927

about 30 painters and decorators employed and there is an office staff of seven clerks."

We can assume that many of those employees were pupils at Barnwell, East Road Boys' School (St George's Church of England Senior Boys' School), situated next to the Girls' and the Infants' Schools between School House Lane (next to Broad Street) and Caroline Place. The new St Matthew's School now occupies the site. A glimpse at the school log book for 1892–1935, which is kept in the Cambridgeshire County Record Office together with the log books of the Senior Girls' School, gives some idea of the social conditions prevalent in the Barnwell area at the turn of the century. There are repeated references to poor attendance at school. Often very bad weather is blamed for the high level of absenteeism. Ill health contributed too. On 14 November 1902 the log book for the Girls' School reads: "Owing to an outbreak of scarlet fever notice has been received from Dr Anningson to close the school for a fortnight." On 28 November the school was told by the medical officer of health to remain closed until after Christmas. In the end it remained

A photograph taken in about 1932 of Samuel Gentle with his family and their spouses. Back row, left to right: Herbert Pamplin, Fred Darler, William Robinson, Kit Pamplin, Jim Nicholson, Con Nicholson, Martha MacKay, Walter Gentle, Duncan MacKay. Middle row: Kate Gentle, Gertrude Robinson, Dan Gentle, Samuel Gentle, May Darler. Front row: Marion Deeks, Sydney Deeks, Ada Gentle

closed for nine weeks, reopening again on 19 January 1903. On 14 May 1907 a "very small attendance yesterday" was attributed to a happier cause: the Scripture Union went on an excursion to Hunstanton. Some 14 years earlier Barnwell, East Road Boys' School had been upset by "St Matthew's Sunday School treat on Tuesday and thunderstorms on Wednesday and today." By October 1893 there was already overcrowding at the school. The entry for 20 October reads: "Admitted 76 boys this week which has made the school very crowded, 397 being present on Tuesday." On 30 April 1914 the Boys' School was closed by order of the Education Authority "in order that the children may see the King as he drives through East Road". On a more sombre note the entry for 13 November 1914 records that "a managers' meeting was held this morning to consider the

advisability of handing over the premises to the military for the purpose of billeting".

Boys playing truant from school in East Road at the turn of the century might have been lured into 13 different alehouses; there were seven on the east side, six on the west. An alley on the east side beyond Norfolk Street was called Brewhouse Lane, and just beyond the Zion Chapel was the Tiger Inn at 5 East Road, later a popular haunt of Arts School staff. Next came the Blackbirds Inn, between Broad Street and School House Lane. It later became the Granville. The Red Lion at no. 50, by the East Road Hall and Free Library Reading Room (Barnwell Branch), was in the stretch of East Road between Norfolk Street and Staffordshire Street. These houses have long since disappeared, and have been replaced by City Council flats designed by the architect David Roberts, probably his one excursion into public housing. It was in the Staffordshire Street/New Street/Gas Lane area that the first bombs fell on Cambridge during the last war. At the corner of Staffordshire Street Mrs Cann ran the George IV at 71 East Road, next door to her bootshop at no. 70. George IV and Caroline Place are East Road's two Regency associations. The George IV was certainly one of the oldest pubs in the road and was probably

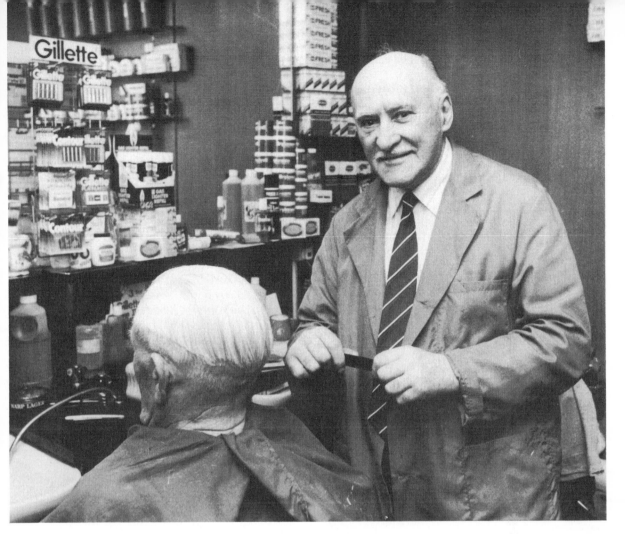

Albert Scott, hairdresser and raconteur

established, together with Caroline Place, early in the 1820s (that's guesswork!). A little further on at no. 80 was the Turnstile (landlord William Gates), two doors away from the Wheelwright's Arms at no. 82, which was next door to the Horse and Jockey. On the opposite side of East Road at no. 119 was the Britannia Inn, next to Britannia Place, one of those little alleys leading off East Road. The Britannia, now pulled down, was a late Georgian pub with a vast shop-front, probably a navvies' pub built to be tough. Architect Jon Harris, who acquired some of the fittings when it was demolished, including the double doors from the front and grand pilasters from along the façade, recalls that the Britannia was "set at a funny angle to the road. It had dome windows like a butterfly-wing arrangement, which sloped downward." Then at 140 East Road was the Three Compasses, next to Compasses Passage. At nos. 153–154 was the Pelican, and further on at no. 170, on the corner of Burleigh Street, was the

Waggon and Horses, now the Falcon. The Baker's Arms at no. 176 is also still there, refurbished. In one of the few surviving sections of Georgian East Road, it is sandwiched between original cottages onto which new frontages have been added. A pub crawl round East Road in 1901 would have finished at the Alhambra, just down from Dover Street, between two shops, a butcher's and a grainer and marbler's.

But there were other drinks than beer to be found in the road. In 1919 you could take tea in Mrs Cockerton's Perseverance Cafe at no. 29 between W. Perry Leach and Son, the art workmen and painting, glazing, metal and cabinet works, and the A.R.C. Knitting Company at no. 30 (which was next door to J. Ward and Son, the cycle agents, now N.J. Thake, the "Cycle King"). And there was a dairy at no. 20, owned by the popular milkman George Anderson. His granddaughter, Mrs Peggy Fletcher of 64 Malvern Road, who was born at the dairy, remembers that her grandfather ran a general shop as well there after the first war. He also owned no. 22, which he let to a watchmaker and jeweller, G.H. Kirkup.

Industrial unrest and poverty in late-19th-century Scotland drove a young man called Donald MacKay south to seek work in England. He and his brothers had trained as engineers in and around the shipyards of Rosyth, and he had had a job as foreman at the Carron Ironworks in Edinburgh, but strikes, lock-outs and violence at the Ironworks had made his situation intolerable. He first tried London, taking with him his children, Duncan and Isabella. No jobs there! It was in Cambridge that he finally found employment, with Laurie and McConnal in Fitzroy Street. He set up home in nearby Christchurch Street, where he was joined by his mother and father and his sister Joan. His grandson ex-mayor Donald MacKay takes up the story. In an article published in the parish magazine of St Andrew's, Cherry Hinton, in March 1983, he writes: "Donald and Duncan soon became the mainstay of Laurie's hardware department and built it up into a thriving

wholesale and retail organisation serving a wide area of East Anglia. Donald was sent to America to bring back ideas for the new department store which continued in existence until quite recently in Fitzroy Street. From Christchurch Street the family moved to 143 Cherry Hinton Road, which the children of the area soon christened 'the bagpipe house' because Donald attracted pipers from all over the place to come and practise with him in his garden." By about 1910 the Scottish directors of Laurie and McConnal, who had worked so well with Donald and Duncan, had retired and left the firm. Duncan and Donald apparently did not see "eye to eye" with the new wave of directors and "made a break for it by buying the wheelwright and fencemaking firm of Alsop and Sons in East Road . . . the deal, it is said, was struck over the anvil, much to the disgust of some of the younger Alsops who had been expecting to take over the business".

Father and son worked hard building up the business in East Road, doing heating installations and millwrighting as well as wheelwrighting. Duncan died in 1936, predeceasing his father, and it was his sister Isabella who inherited the firm when their father died in 1943. Her nephew Donald, Duncan's

Pupils of Miss Thompson's class at New Street School in 1920. Albert Scott is second from the right in the second row from the front

JAMES ROLFE.
Licensed to sell Beer & Tobacco to be consumed on the Premises

GOOD LODGINGS FOR SINGLE MEN

TEBBUTT'S | ALES & STOU

The Horse and Jockey public house, in about 1912. Fourth from the right is Soopy Barratt, the rat-catcher

son, remembers that "all the intervening years she had been a school teacher in Birmingham but she retrained herself to run the firm while the next generation were growing up. In due course she took Duncan's son and eldest daughter Joan into partnership in the firm. At the age of 90 Isabella was still in harness in the family business making up wage packets, dealing with PAYE and coping with all manner of financial matters." She was loved by everyone in the firm. A master craftswoman in silver and gold whose Limoges enamel miniatures had received acclaim in London and Europe, Isabella MacKay taught patients at the tuberculosis settlement at Papworth to do basketwork and handicraft during the first world war. It was from this germ of an idea that the Papworth Industries developed.

Donald MacKay, who now runs the family business with his sister Mrs Joan Moore, was born at 62 Abbey Road. He told me of his early memories of that part of Barnwell. "We were totally banned from crossing Newmarket Road and going to East Road because it was a rough place in the 1930s. Father got beaten up one night on his way home

from work." But the MacKay children were taken over to East Road to visit their maternal grandparents, Samuel and Maria Gentle. Samuel Gentle was a coal merchant and carter, who had his business first at 85a and then at 95 East Road. Donald MacKay, whose mother was born Martha Gentle, remembers the Gentle yard as a haven. "The house was at the gates, while down the yard there were places where they stored hay and sacks of coal. There was a stables at the bottom." The Gentles were a well-known Barnwell family. Six of the Gentle daughters married men connected with local businesses. Kit married Herbert Pamplin, who was in charge of the furniture department at Laurie and McConnal. Fred Darler, who married May, was the baker at 47 New Street; William Robinson, who married Gertrude, was transport manager at Chivers; and Sydney Deeks, who married Marion, worked for Cambridgeshire Motors. And of the Gentle sons, Walter ran the corn, coal and forage business with his father Samuel, while his brother Dan was a director of J.A. Sturton Ltd, the tea blenders of Fitzroy Street. Duncan MacKay, husband of Martha, was known in sporting circles as Sonny. He was a boxer, swimmer and cyclist.

Next door to Gentle's Yard was Swann's Yard.

H.A. Swann Bros Ltd were lime burners, as well as sand and gravel merchants and pit owners. The lime (forerunner of cement in the building industry) came from Lime Kiln Hill in Cherry Hinton, and was mixed with sand to make mortar. Marlow and Co., timber and builders' merchants, took over the yard from Swann's, but now MacKays own the premises: it is their metal warehouse. Iron rings in the wall recall the horse-drawn age.

Cambridge tramway fanatics will be quick to remind me that nothing recalls the horse-drawn era in East Road more obviously than the dilapidated old depot of the Cambridge Street Tramway Company (founded 1879) at the junction of East Road and Dover Street. Since the last war the depot has been the property of George Peak the furniture removers, who have used it for storage. When Mr Peak bought the building in 1945 it was still the old coach house, though the Tramway Company ceased operations in 1918. The tramlines are no longer there; some have been taken up and sent to an East Midlands transport museum. The windows visible from East Road were those of the hayloft.

The Barnwell rat-catcher, the cress seller, the barrel organ tuner from the Britannia Yard and the tripe and onion man are just a few characters in East Road remembered by barber Albert Scott, who was born at 120 East Road on 2 March 1913. Barnwell's entrepreneurs, forced by poverty and unemployment to have a go at anything, are steeped in country lore. Listening to Albert Scott bring them to life, you can almost hear the clattering in the yard at the Britannia Inn where publican and shoesmith Joe Day did the shoeing for the old Star Brewery in Newmarket Road, and smell the stench from the Castle Soap Factory in Young Street. (Whenever they began to boil up, remembers a former pupil of New Street School, his headmaster would make a dash to close the windows.) The more sensitive and squeamish readers, who can't stomach the thought of Winton Smith's slaughterhouse off Nelson Street or the aroma of tripe and trotters brewed up in a lean-to at the back of Britannia Yard by an old boy called Jones, may prefer to appreciate the talents of Mr Scott's maternal grandfather, Mr Huntly, who repaired billiard tables in Sturton Street, and was noted for his harp playing.

Albert Scott, once a pupil at the New Street School, can people the local alleyways and passageways and the East Road pubs, most of which have been erased from the map, with a host of tenacious survivors, mostly men with large families to feed – his father, also Albert Scott, born in 1888, was the youngest of 16. Mr Scott's barber's shop is the little cottage with the bow window and the distinctive

pole at 169 East Road. He used to give shaves and haircuts "on tick" in anticipation of payment after the regular visit to the pawnbroker. The pawnbrokers in Fitzroy Street did brisk business, particularly on a Monday. "Monday was the day when people in the area took their possessions in to pledge. It was usually a suit which they would take out at the end of the week." At other times he would receive payment in kind. "There was Harry Bradford of Crispin Passage, a rare old boy who lived till over 80 and died full of beer. He sold watercress from a barrow, cress which he got from the local brooks fed by the Nine Wells, where some of the best drinking water comes from. We used to shave him every other day and receive cress in lieu of payment."

In the days before the safety razor was invented men went to the barber for a shave. "You made your living by shaving, not by cutting hair," said Albert. "They were all regulars and had their own shaving pots." The hairdressing side of the business was unisex then. "We had ladies and gents mixed together then and no one thought anything of it." 169 East Road is the oldest established hairdresser's in Cambridge. It began as a barber's in 1826. Albert Scott's father worked with the hairdresser, Mr Loker. When Mr Loker sold the business Albert's father was sold with it as "a pudding improver", which must be a reference to the pudding basin hairstyle. Albert Scott Snr later moved up to 120 East Road, starting his own business there in a shop which his mother rented for him for half a crown a week. Albert Scott Jnr took over the business in 1946. What did a visit to the hairdresser cost in the early days? Albert (who gave Barnwell raconteur Fred ("Pimbo") Unwin his first haircut) has a Cambridge Hairdressers' Association rule book for 1914 which sets out the prices. "Members shall not charge less than 1½d for shaving, 3d for Gents Hair Cut, 2d for schoolboys (under 14 years), 3d for shampooing, and 3d for selling razors. Any member to be allowed to charge 6d per week for shaving only." Albert remembers that a shave and neck shave called a "Boston" cost 3d some 50 years ago.

From his intimate connection with Barnwell life stretching over more than 70 years Albert Scott can remember men like Soopy Barratt, the well-known Barnwell rat-catcher, who seemed to be more successful as a rabbit-catcher than as a Pied Piper. "He always had a rabbit in his pocket," says Albert. Other people may remember Mrs Lefley, who lived two doors down from the Horse and Jockey opposite the Britannia. She was noted for her pickle making – "all home made" – and for laying on a bowl of peas and a bread roll for a penny when the

The Working Men's Club in East Road before it was demolished

men came out of the Britannia at closing time. Round at the Wheelwright's Arms the landlord R.V. Hall, like other publicans, took in lodgers. One of his visitors arrived with a huge performing bear, which Albert Scott remembers was kept in the sheds at the back.

For more than 35 years Albert Scott has been a trustee of the Cambridge Working Men's Club and Institute. He is its oldest member. The club was established in 1873, and until Grosvenor Estates developed the Grafton Centre it stood at the junction of Fitzroy Street and East Road. Now in temporary premises in Occupation Road, it is being rebuilt further up East Road, 20 yards from its old site. The club's 1901 rule book sets out the objects of the institute: "to afford to the industrial classes the means of social intercourse, mutual helpfulness, mental and moral improvement and rational recreation . . . Membership is open to any person above the age of 18 on being proposed by a member and being elected by the committee, by paying a subscription of one shilling per quarter in advance and agreeing to abide by the rules." The club provided cards for members to play whist, cribbage, and "Don". "The loser of each game shall pay one halfpenny to the club funds", says the rule book.

It was a Mr and Miss Hopkins who saw the need for such a club and institute. In 1863 they began to collect subscriptions and issued a circular setting out their plans "to erect a small Workmen's Hall, where members would be provided with coffee, books, newspapers and any quiet and proper amusement. Accommodation will be afforded for lectures, read-

ing classes and singing classes." The cost of the enterprise was estimated at between £700 and £800. The site was bought for £80 from Jesus College, but the building eventually cost £1,280. On the top floor, says Mr Stanley Brown of High Street, Teversham, whose grandfather was landlord of the Britannia in the 1870s, was a theatre called The People's Theatre, which put on two shows a week – rip-roaring melodramas like *Maria Marten and the Red Barn* and *Sweeny Todd the Demon Barber* went down especially well. At one time the club had 1,000 members; now it has between 800 and 900 who get together for socials, bingo and monthly "kneesups". The club (which is non-political) is still an important part of Barnwell's social framework.

The Cambridgeshire College of Arts and Technology (CCAT, pronounced "cat" or "sea cat"), which occupies the large site between Mill Road Cemetery and East Road, originated as a 19th-century art school, one of the first in the country. John Ruskin, the great art critic (*Stones of Venice*, etc., etc.), who had so strongly sponsored the development of art schools, gave the inaugural address. 20th-century artists who have studied there and been associated with it include Ronald Searle and Edward Bawden. Now one of the major centres of the study and practice of illustration in this country, the Art School enjoys strong links with Cambridge University Press and other local publishers (the University Printer is a Governor). Recent graduates include the Cambridge-based team Peter Fluck and Roger Law, inventors of the three-dimensional cartoon and the ITV series "Spitting Image".

The original School opened at 9 Sidney Street on 1 November 1858. There were classes for Ladies (Elementary and Advanced) and for Gentlemen

A view of the Cambridgeshire College of Art and Technology's new building on East Road

(Advanced) in the morning, and in the evening there was a Gentlemen's Special Class and an Artisans' Class. Artisans paid 2 shillings a month and Gentlemen and Ladies 5 shillings. The School was maintained by voluntary subscriptions, fees and a government grant, and was run by a committee of subscribers. An anonymous history of the first hundred years of CCAT, *The Cambridgeshire Technical College and School of Art 1858–1958*, explains that by 1862 the School had moved to special rooms in the Guildhall. "In 1889, a few years after the appearance of industrial depression for the first time since the founding of the School, the Technical Instruction Act was passed, a sign of the recognition of the need to improve technical education to meet the new German challenge." The result was that the Cambridge Borough Council made an annual grant of £100 and built a small Institute for Technical

Education in East Road. An account in the history of a Cambridge student at the Institute gives a picture of late Victorian life in Cambridge outside the University. "He was an apprentice around the turn of the century earning two and sixpence a week in the building trade, working from six in the morning to half-past five at night and then going along in the evening to what is now the Drill Hall in East Road where there were classes in Building Construction, Architectural Drawing, Woodwork and Wood Carving." As the history says, "such a self-imposed discipline must have weeded out the reluctant student". There was also a hut off East Road where there were classes in other subjects, including cookery. (The Drill Hall, with its fine copper coat of arms, now belongs to the Post Office. It was used for many years by the Territorial Army and was also the venue for local gatherings and dances.)

CCAT's Collier Road site (open fields until mid-Victorian times) was opened in 1909 by the American ambassador, Whitelaw Reid. The Education Act of 1921 which pioneered day continuation schools emphasised the need for systematic technical education. The 1926 prospectus of the Cambridge and County School of Arts, Crafts and Technology lists Departments of Fine and Applied Arts, Commerce, Domestic Crafts, Technology and Science, and Language and Literature; Continuation Classes provided courses for apprentices in the building, printing and retail trades and in scientific laboratories. Expansion at the School continued between the wars. The numbers of part-time day students increased from 50 in 1921 to 130 in 1930, while the numbers of evening students went up from 253 to 1,106. In 1921 there were 15 full-time students; by 1930, 117. These full-time students were pupils in the Day Trade School section which trained boys and girls for employment in skilled industries – although with the recession in the 1930s job prospects in these areas were bleak. The Trade School offered courses in building, commerce, cookery, dressmaking, engineering, printing and woodwork. Students entered at the age of 14, staying two years and spending about one-third of their time on their trade and the remainder on general studies. During the second world war the College carried out contract work for the Government and acted as a trainee department for the Ministry of Labour, as well as carrying on its teaching role.

The growth in student numbers and the wide range of courses have always meant pressure on accommodation. The site was expanded to cope with the growing demands. The original Edwardian red brick building was shared with the County Girls' School (it is recorded that the connecting door was out of bounds). Another wing was added in 1925 and this was further extended in 1931, and then at the outbreak of war the girls were moved to Long Road and the College took over their rooms. Prefabs first appeared in 1947, before more solid buildings were constructed in 1956 and 1958. Building has continued ever since. By 1958, the year of its centenary, the College had more than 500 full-time students and more than 5,000 part-time, together with a staff of over 100 and 300 visiting specialists.

A big breakthrough took place in the early 1970s when the old London External Degree started to disappear and CNAA (Council for National Academic Awards) degrees were introduced. The first CNAA degree was in modern languages. Then followed humanities and sociology (HumSoc), English, history, science, geography and more recently electronic engineering, for of course the Tech is into hi-tech! The building of the Mumford Theatre and auditorium was one of the highspots of the 1970s developments. Last autumn the large new block replacing temporary accommodation was opened on East Road next to the Zion Chapel; the builders were the East Road firm of Coulsons. In the 125 years since its tiny beginnings in Sidney Street, the College has become a major centre for advanced technological, professional and cultural education. Let's hope it can stay that way despite the recent cuts.

21 Grafton Street

21 April 1983

Grafton Street, named after John Grafton, who brought gas to Cambridge, rather than after the duke, was once the home of artisans who formed the backbone of Cambridge and the University. Now it has been gentrified – Liberal councillors, successful businessmen and retired couples are among the new "villagers" who live in this desirable, reprieved part of the Kite.

Grafton Street is an early Victorian street, probably post-1845 – one of the last streets to be built on the large market garden known as The Garden of Eden (see Eden Street). That part of the Kite, an area of 17 acres, was allotted to James Burleigh by the Enclosure Commissioners on 4 February 1812. Burleigh sold the land to Thomas Palmer of Ely for £1,259 in 1820. When Thomas Palmer died in 1831 he left the land to his widow, Mary Lucas Palmer. Two years later she married Thomas George Gifford and sold off part of the freehold land which she had inherited from her first husband. Presumably after that the land was sold off in small lots to speculative builders.

One of the first houses to be built in the street was a hotel at no. 38, the Suffolk Hotel; it was a small coaching inn with a great many bedrooms. Horses would have been tethered in the yard at the back and drink stored in the large cellars below. According to street directory entries, it ceased to operate as a hotel soon after the turn of the century and became a private house. Now it is the home of Mr Kenneth Sewell and his Belgian wife Tuulikki, who have patiently fashioned one large house out of two adjacent ones, nos. 38 and 39. Relics of the Suffolk Hotel exist in the form of *fin de siècle* wall paintings of nubile, languid ladies.

Nos. 4–7 Grafton Street make an interesting group – they have the look of almshouses. Jack Lang, a director of the computer firm Top Express, lives at no. 4, and he wonders whether they were agricultural buildings. They are built out of square ashlar blocks which could have come from the fabric of Cambridge Castle, demolished in the 1840s. These four houses are considered sufficiently distinguished to merit an entry by the Royal Commission on Historical Monuments, which dates them round about 1850 and refers to their "exotic arrangement of pilasters and half-pilasters" and, on the first floor, their "panels containing stucco blank shields, Renaissance grotesques in oval medallions and wooden crosses *flory*". In 1874 they were inhabited by a policeman, a painter, a brewer's man and a boot closer – not obvious candidates for almshouses, but there is a cottagey atmosphere about these houses; indeed the whole area is quite a village. Jack Lang, who is fond of cooking, has planted 60 varieties of herbs in his garden at the back. Angelica, cowslip, comfrey and rosemary flourish there. He is one of a group of about 20 people who are cultivating an allotment on derelict land in Paradise Street.

The CCAT Advanced Students' Club occupies a large Victorian building designed by the architect W.M. Fawcett for the Jesus Lane Sunday School, which started life in the Quaker Meeting House in Jesus Lane. The school moved from Jesus Lane to schoolrooms in King Street in 1833, but premises became cramped and it was decided to build a new Sunday School in the parish of St Andrew the Less. A building committee considered a site in Prospect Row, but finally decided in favour of the present site. An extensive garden in Paradise Street was purchased in 1865, and a large two-storey building was built by the firm of Quinsee and Attack. The school had a frontage on Grafton Street and occupied the stretch of land between Paradise Street and Grafton Street. On the Grafton Street frontage can be seen the inscription "J.L.S.S. 1827–77". The history of the Jesus Lane Sunday School by Charles Alfred Jones records that the new building was opened on 31 October 1867 with a public meeting presided over by the Vice-Chancellor. The building in Grafton Street provided the Sunday School with a large, well-lit room nearly 60 ft in length and breadth. Youth clubs called the Albert Institute used the ground floor as reading rooms and classrooms. At the beginning of 1871 the large room on

A poster advertising houses for sale in Grafton Street in 1852

4 NEW BUILT HOUSES

GRAFTON ROAD, GARDEN OF EDEN
CAMBRIDGE.

TO BE SOLD BY AUCTION, BY

CHAS. WISBEY,

At the Black Birds Public House, East Road,
On THURSDAY, 8th of July, 1852,

AT SEVEN O'CLOCK IN THE EVENING.

LOT 1. A well-built Brick and Slate HOUSE, at the corner of Adam & Eve Row, containing Five Rooms and Shop, and Yard at the back, with pair of Folding Gates, as now occupied by Mr. GAUTREY, at the yearly Rent of £12.

LOT 2. A newly finished Brick and Slate House adjoining, containing 4 Rooms, and a detached wash-house, with Garden behind, having a back entrance (at present unoccupied.)

LOT 3. A similar House & Premises adjoining.

LOT 4. A detatched Brick and Slate HOUSE, containing Four Rooms, large Wash-house, and Yard at the back, with side entrance, as occupied by Mrs. RICKARD, at the yearly Rent of £9. 9s.

N.B. The Passage between Lots 3 and 4, is common to Lots 2, 3, and 4.

All the above are FREEHOLD, and Land Tax redeemed. The HOUSES are all well-built, and are fitted up with Grates, Coppers, and Cupboards.

Further particulars may be known of Mr. PEED, Solicitor; or of CHARLES WISBEY, Auctioneer, Valuer, and Estate Agent, Sidney Street, Cambridge.

LADDS & CO., PRINTERS, HOBSON'S PLACE, CAMBRIDGE.

Nos. 4–7 Grafton Street, with their unusual decoration

the first floor and some of the lower rooms were let to the Higher Grade Boys' School. A Cricket Club used the classrooms too, instead of convening at a public house, and a temperance association held its meetings there in its early days. In the 1930s the building was sold to the Scouts.

Nos. 16, 17, 18 and 20, 21 and 21a were late additions to the housing stock of Grafton Street. They were under construction in 1911 and built in the gaps between nos. 15 and 19 and 19 and 22 on what had been the large garden of no. 19. No. 17 is the home of Liberal councillors Colin and Joyce Rosenstiel, who moved there from York Street. Election posters in the window remind us all that the May local elections are on the way. Councillor Chris Bradford called with canvass cards while I was there. He and the Rosenstiels are campaigning hard for Lavena Hawes.

At the corner of Grafton Street and Adam and Eve Street on the north side stands Grafton House. Its new owners, Chester and Liz White, are involved in a large-scale restoration job on what was considered to be one of the most gracious houses in the street. For many years it was the home of a dressmaker, Miss Alice Bilton. No. 23 has gone. It used to be the Grafton Arms, a Star Brewery pub. It was demolished in the early 1970s, and no. 24, the house next door, was demolished at the same time. But renovation rather than demolition is what is happening now in Grafton Street. Houses are in demand there, and one which had recently been "done up" has just sold for a figure in the region of £38,500.

22 City Road

23 July 1981

This little street of artisan dwellings in the shadow of the Kite was built in the 1840s for local factory workers. The industrial association probably gave it its name of City Road, and it retains the homogeneous atmosphere for which it has traditionally been renowned.

Once the home of carpenters, painters, tailors, grocers, bakers, commercial travellers and college servants, whose wives by their diligence with the elbow grease would have ensured a prize in the best-kept street award had there been such a thing 100 years ago, City Road is quietly coming to life again now that the planning blight has been lifted. People may not be polishing their window sills or brightening up their shoe scrapers as they did when Mrs Hilda Desborough's father, John Summerlin, kept the bakery at 23 City Road at the turn of the century, but they are persisting with the window-boxes and hanging baskets, in spite of having them kicked down the street or stuffed with fish and chip papers.

Parts of City Road have become totally gentrified in the last ten years. Academics, professional people, artists and young families have made some of these humble little cottages, the most unassuming of which can fetch around £25,000, into individual nests. Mrs Desborough, who is married to a farmer and lives at Elsworth, told me that in her day, the people of City Road "knew where every spider had its web" – her phrase for having roots in a village-like community. She might be pleasantly surprised by the rejuvenation of City Road today. It is becoming a highly respectable street about which people talk with unabashed enthusiasm. Antoinette Moses, director of Cambridge's Animation Festival, moved to 10 City Road from London two years ago. "I love this street. It is like a village with a marvellous community feeling," she said. Lady Wheeler, widow of Sir Mortimer Wheeler, has also recently moved into the street.

Let's take a pre-war trip around City Road with Hilda Desborough who was born at no. 23 in 1910. "I had a wonderful childhood there. My mother was Miss Mary Louisa Start of Thompsons Lane. She married father who was an apprentice baker to Mr

W.H. Bennett of 23 City Road. Father took over the bakery in 1894." Mr Summerlin was a good baker who used to win prizes for his Hovis. Mrs Des-

Scharlie Wraight and Stephen Platt transforming the Cambridge Friendly Society building into the Eden Centre of Dance

Harold Lister, "a cabinet maker of the old school"

borough remembers that the bakehouse was round the corner in John Street. "The bottom half of the bakehouse window was whitewashed to stop people looking in. Fourteen steps led down to the cellar." Mr Summerlin's ovens were always full. The people of City Road used to take their meat, their turkeys at Christmas, their hams and any other special meals over to him to cook in his ovens. He had his special orders too. "My father baked all the bread for Clare College and also made bread for royalty," says Mrs Desborough proudly.

Mr Summerlin wasn't the only baker in City Road in those days. There was Mr Digby too. He had his bakery on the corner of City Road and Grafton Street. It is now the premises of the Cambridge Engraving Company, which has been in City Road for 17 years. The old oven is bricked in at the back of the workshop where Mr Brian George and his partner Mr Eric Richardson engrave everything from instrument panels for Tornado aircraft to walkie-talkie pocket radios used by the police.

In Mrs Desborough's day the east side of City Road, starting from the Forester's pub, was a mixture of private houses and shops. "There were private houses as far as the Paradise Street corner. Mrs Nancy Maltby, the sub-postmistress of the Fitzroy Street post office which used to be where Morleys are now, lived on the corner. On the other corner of Paradise Street and City Road was Goldings, the dairy. They sold milk and greengroceries." That was 8 City Road. It is now the showroom and workshop of Kingsway Motorcycles Ltd, who as well as their obvious trade in motorcycles do a nice little sideline in seasonal produce. Last week, they were selling fresh cos lettuce for 5p, and strawberries at 35p a pound. Mrs Desborough also recalls the hat shop which Miss Nora Leach ran from her home next door to Digbys the bakers. "Miss Leach used to make her hats on moulds. My mother got all her hats there." No. 21 used to be the home of Mr and Mrs Howard. Mr Howard was a retired carpenter, his wife was Mrs Desborough's great-aunt, born Emma Summerlin.

On the opposite corner of John Street and City Road lived Mr and Mrs Linsell, in a house which local residents believe was a pub many years ago. Mr Linsell was a carpenter at the New Theatre and he and his wife used to let rooms to what locals called "the theatricals" from the theatre. Mr Lever, a decorator, had his workshop on the opposite side of City Road, opposite Brandon Court. Next came a little shoe shop and cobblers. It adjoined three bay-windowed houses, nos. 25a, b and c. A flat at the back of 25a City Road is now the home of BBC journalist Mr Tom Wisdom. In the old days Mr and Mrs Howlett kept a general stores at no. 25b. They used to sell everything from bacon to firewood – you could buy two bundles of firewood for three farthings. The Misses Holder at 26 City Road remember the lovely pats of roly poly butter which Mr Howlett specialised in. As children, Miss Nora and Miss Florence Holder lived at 32 City Road. Their father was a University Bulldog and worked at Clare College. He and their mother died when the sisters were quite young, and their uncle and aunt, Mr and Mrs Sam Maltby, took the girls to live with them at no. 26. Mr Maltby was a gyp at Clare College and his son, George, worked at Clare as well.

Miss Nora Holder was in service for many years with Miss Eleanor Rolleston, the cousin of Sir

Eric Richardson at the Cambridge Engraving Company

Humphrey Rolleston, whose great-uncle invented the Davy Safety Lamp. Miss Rolleston lived in a large house in Fitzwilliam Road. Miss Florence Holder worked as a tailoress for Palmers the tailor in Green Street. The garden of 26 City Road is pretty but minute, and it is overshadowed by the back of Millers in Eden Street. What happened to the original garden? The story goes that during the war, Mr Maltby was persuaded to sell part of it to Mr Suttle the tailor, who lived in Eden Street. Mr Suttle desperately wanted to build an air-raid shelter to protect his daughters. Mr Maltby was a kind-hearted man, but the sale cost him a large chunk of the garden which his nieces greatly miss today.

Leach the joiner had his joinery works at 27 City Road. Mrs Desborough used to keep angora rabbits in the yard of their home at no. 23, and she got sawdust for them from Mr Leach. To continue the game of City Road's Happy Families, we would have come to 28 City Road where Cleverley, the jeweller, was in business. He was apparently a very frightening man with a grey beard. He was very stern but his niece loved children. Mr and Mrs Wolston lived next door. Their son, Sid, was a general odd-job man. His brother, Stanley, kept an antique shop in St Andrew's Street which Queen Mary used to visit. Mr Harold Lister, the popular local carpenter and joiner who trained at John Brignell's, has lived at 35 City Road since 1941. His workshop is under the arch at nos. 36 and 37, properties which are in trust to the Catholic Church. "This used to be the paintshop of F.R. Leach and his son Barnett, the painters and church decorators," Mr Lister told me. "F.R. Leach started the business there in 1850, and at one time had 60 painters based here who went all over the country." Mr Lister, a cabinet maker of the old school, has a little stained glass window of Pre-Raphaelite delicacy hanging in his workshop. There are other legacies of Leach work in other studios on the site. Artist Edwin Mortlock has a studio there. Upstairs over Mr Lister is Screens and Graphics, silk screen processors. City Road has maintained its tradition as a street of small craft-based industries. I would call it the street of skills.

Opposite Paradise Street there was once a pub called the Coopers Arms. It was kept in Mrs Desborough's time by a Mr and Mrs Warboys. In 1874, according to the street directory, the landlord was a Thomas Loft. You can see the letters "AD" on the door of 41 City Road. They stand for artisan dwelling, and indicate the origin of the street. Mrs Mary Wraith, who bought no. 41 for £3,500 20 years ago, said that it was then a condemned street. Her house was scheduled for demolition, but she took the risk and was rewarded for her hunch that bureaucracy might change things. Mrs Wraith lists the advantages of living in City Road: you don't need a car, you can walk everywhere and Parkside Community College, with its range of adult evening classes, is a minute's walk away. Mrs Wraith's neighbour, who lived at no. 42 until she died, was "a marvellous old Irish lady called Mrs Aldhouse. She had cooked for the Master of one of the colleges, her husband had been the butler at the Union Society. They had met when he was a footman in a house where she was cook. She was a wonderful neighbour, who would even climb over the wall to bring me presents, saying 'over the top and the best of luck to you'." Mrs Wraith also remembers the late Mrs Lister, wife of Mr Harold Lister, who performed many kindnesses in the street. "She was an ex-nursing sister who was often called in to help people."

Perhaps the greatest metamorphosis in City Road has been the transformation of no. 47, formerly the Cambridge Friendly Society building, into the Eden Centre of Dance. Dancer Maureen Singh, who has been teaching for eight years, and her partners Scharlie Wraight and Stephen Platt learned basic building skills to turn squatter-damaged premises, riddled with dry rot, into heated dance studios with an expanse of mirrors on the wall. The exterior is gaunt, but the interior has rooms on a splendid scale – they are the two studios – and a noble staircase. Renovation and reconstruction continues with plans to enlarge changing rooms and convert a large cellar into a coffee bar. Meanwhile, as well as all the dance classes for children and adults that go on there, the studios are for hire for shows, fashion photography and rehearsals. It would be a splendid venue for anyone wanting large rooms for a meeting or show. Mrs Singh lives at no. 46, in the house that belonged to the caretaker of the Forester's. No. 49, until recently let to the Cyrenians, is to become a Church Army House.

That just about concludes our walk round City Road. We end, of course, at Thompsons the furniture shop on the corner of Fitzroy Street. They used to have horse-drawn carts in the old days, which they kept at the end of John Street. No doubt the carriers would have refreshed themselves at the Forester's pub over the road, where landlord Mr John Barrett is proud to show anyone who is interested a blown-up photograph taken in 1908 of the pub as it used to be. The exterior hasn't changed much, it is Burleigh Street behind that has. It is nice that City Road isn't changing drastically and that it has retained its scale. It is an interesting street, and now the Fitzroy Street end has been included in the Prospect Row Improvement Area.

23 Eden Street

19 February 1981

A visitor to Cambridge at the turn of the century might have been struck by the number of tailors finding their living in the City.

Take Eden Street, that little jewel of a street, folded into the edge of the poor, battered old Kite like an unobtrusive tuck which the unpicking scissors have missed. According to the street directory for 1874, there were 17 tailors living in the street, including five seamstresses. Imagine it! The area must have been the Spitalfields of Cambridge, with families earning their living by the needle. Colleges would have been the major customers, with all their linen requirements – the sheets, the bedding, the tablecloths and, of course, the gowns for the "young gentlemen". It's not so long ago since Mr Leslie Suttle ran his clothing factory in what used to be the Girls' Higher Grade School in Eden Street. The building is now a warehouse and workshop for Kitchen 22. Leslie Suttle's father, Mr Frank Suttle, started the business about 70 years ago in Fitzroy Street. And Mrs Ida Casey, who was born in 7 Eden Street, where she lives with her husband George, told me that her father was a tailor in Rose Crescent. "My mother was a worker at Emmanuel College. As well as going in the morning, she used to go back again in the evening to turn down the beds and wash up the tea things." Mr and Mrs Casey both worked at Hawkins' bakery in Parsonage Street, and Mr Casey remembers when there were 70 pubs in the Kite area.

The whole of the Kite evolved through the industriousness of the successful, immensely hard-

Looking down Eden Street to Fitzroy Street

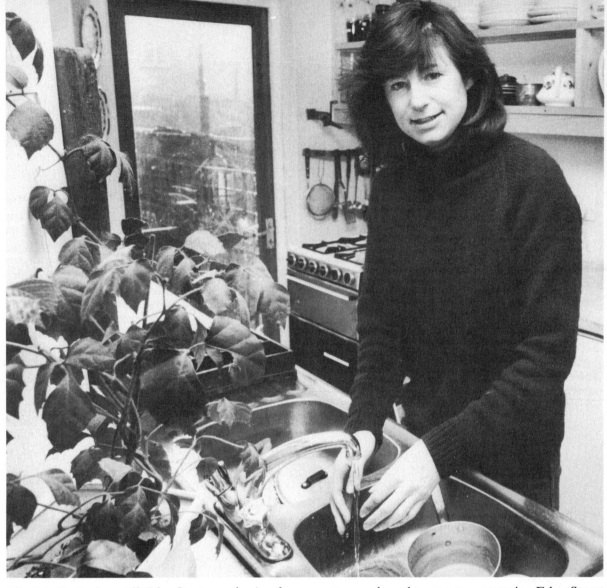

Mrs Priscilla Bridger at 52 Eden Street over the site of a Tudor well

working artisans of the 19th century. It was their quarter, they developed it through imaginative local builders with the cohesion of style which we can still see in parts. Nowhere in the Kite is this attention to architectural harmony better illustrated than in the unique workman's terrace on the west side of Eden Street (the whole side is the property of Jesus College). Conservationists sigh with relief to know that each cottage is deemed a listed building by the Department of the Environment, and that the whole street, with the exception of one or two properties at the Fitzroy Road end (the eczema on the face of the street), is included in the Prospect Row Improvement Area.

But back first to the open fields of the early 19th century, when the area encompassing Eden Street was known romantically as the Garden of Eden. It was one big market garden. The neighbouring streets – Paradise Street, Adam and Eve Street, Prospect Row, Elm Street (was the elm then the Tree of Knowledge?) – also reflect this reliance on the Scriptures. You can't get much further back than the Creation, but the estates bursar of Jesus College, Mr John Mills, kindly dug into the college muniments room to give me the history of their side of the street, where in recent years so much dramatic rehabilitation of the interiors of the cottages has been taking place, at no small expense to the college. This is the story.

"We got the land there with the Barnwell enclosure award of 1809. At that time, in 1822, it was known as Gravel Close. It was in lease until 1822, probably being used for agricultural purposes. The first homes were built about 1833–4, the land being leased out to building developers. Barretts, the china family, were one of the first leasees. They were 40-year leases, and they were renewed over a period of years. Most of them came back to the college in 1900." Was there an architect for the row? Mr Mills put it like this: "There was no architect, the style and symmetry were just the good manners of the time. They were built very cheaply, but we have no record of who built them. Probably the developers got together and employed the same builder, who then built three or four houses together."

The harmony of the west side of Eden Street, known in the 1830s as Love Lane, is matched on the other side of the road by a pleasing mix of architectural styles. The earliest houses are late Regency. A street map of 1832 shows what was to become Eden Street in the 1850s as a track through the Garden of Eden to what is now Fitzroy Street. Three houses are shown on the east side of what is Eden Street today. Anthony and Sally Jones, who live at no. 49, believe that their house was the first to be built in the street. Anthony Jones, who runs the Period Piece antique shop at 15 Gwydir Street, is busy restoring his Eden Street home to its original Georgian state. There is a lovely staircase, wide floorboards, and a set of wall paintings of flowers which have come to light in the hall and front room and are believed to be the work of the man who built the house about 1820, Edward Martin Kempton, a painter and grainer.

The rest of Eden Street was built in the Victorian era, so the east side is a mixture of low and high. From the simple Georgian house your eye will travel along, and up to, say, a Victorian three-storey house with a basement, and then back in time to an earlier terrace, just before the Kitchen 22 buildings. The state of certain Council properties, however, leaves a lot to be desired, both externally and internally. Rotting refuse in basement areas is more than a blot, it's a health hazard.

The older generation hark back nostalgically to the days when, as Mr Bill Metcalfe of no. 25 puts it, "it used to be the best little old street in Cambridge". Mr Metcalfe, who came to the street when he was 27, recalls the days of the horse and cart. "I can remember the old fruiterer 'Bowey' Odell. He used to come up here with his horse and cart shouting 'tomatis, tomatis!'." Mr John Price, a retired builder, has lived at no. 57 since 1947. The house was a condemned property then, but being a builder he was able to put it to rights. He takes a tougher line on changes in the street. "The street has changed a lot since I've been here. The people used to be the older, respected people who kept themselves more as citizens should do. In latter years we have had all sorts."

Mr Price was a pupil at the old Higher Grade School (now Parkside Community College). He first went to it in 1924 and remembers the segregation of the boys and girls. "They were two entirely separate schools with separate entrances. There was no stepping over the forbidden line in the middle of the lawn." Mr Price used to cycle into school every day from Landbeach. "My father was a time-serving soldier for 19 years. After he left the Army, he trained as a watch and clock repairer and ran his own business in Landbeach. All his sons, myself and two brothers, worked in the building trade and after the war we started up our own business together." Mr Casey says that the boys from the Higher Grade School had to behave "like young gentlemen" when they walked down Eden Street because "our second headmaster and one of the masters used to lodge at Eden House".

Another pupil at the Higher Grade School was Miss Peggie Temple of 55 Eden Street. Miss Temple, who ran the florist's shop in the street for over 50 years, retiring in the late 1970s, recalls her schooldays with great clarity. Domestic science formed a key part of the curriculum. For their laundry lessons on Monday the girls went to the Council domestic science and handicrafts centre in what used to be the Girls' Higher Grade School in Eden Street (that school was closed down in 1913). "We would spend all day there on a Monday, washing in the morning and ironing all afternoon. One week it was woollens, another week tablecloths and linens or towels. For the finest pillow our teacher used to give the girl one shilling. Because I lived near I used to be responsible for getting the clothes dry so they could be ironed in the afternoon."

Miss Temple was preparing to go and play the piano at a monthly service at Brandon Court when I called to see her. She was happy to talk about the days when she used to help her father in the florist's shop, and then latterly when she ran the shop herself. Funerals were a particularly busy time for them. "I remember when Lord Rutherford died, we did a lot of wreaths for his funeral. And when anyone died at the Fair, my goodness, we were busy. I remember a young girl dying, her grave is the first in the cemetery at Newmarket Road, and all the Fair people came in for flowers." Miss Temple's shop used to be Funge's, the baker's, and she has built her garden on what used to be the bakehouse floor. "I've got a back way into City Road. This is the way the pony used to come to the bakery, and there used to be a hayloft above the stables at the back. Mr King opposite at no. 30 was a character. He was a

At Constable's Glass Works. Left to right: Colin Browne, the late Dennis Anderson and Roy Driver

fireman. He always left his bicycle outside so that he could go off when the bell sounded outside his house summoning him to a fire. When it rang, out he'd come and off he'd go down to St Andrew's Street. When he died, I was only a little girl, but I remember they put the coffin on the tender. I watched from my bedroom window and saw the fire engine covered in flowers."

Just up from Miss Temple lives one of the newcomers to the street, Mrs Priscilla Bridger, at no. 52 – that's the tall Victorian house. Mrs Bridger, a member of the Kite Community Action committee, is another local resident who is fascinated by the history of the street as well as appreciative of all its current amenities. "It's a lovely street, pubs up that end, shops up the other. I find it very friendly." When the Bridgers were rebuilding the extension at the back of their house, they found an old Tudor well built of curved bricks. It was full of mud and water. Antiquarians came in to have a look before it was covered up under the new extension. The distinguished etcher Juliet de Gaye is another newcomer to Eden Street. She and her bloodhound Charlie moved into no. 62 from North Yorkshire, when weavers Paul Clough and Anna Cady moved up to Scotland. Why did she choose Eden Street? "I had always loved Cambridge. I decided I wanted to find a little house with a large studio. Everyone said I was mad, that I would never find one in the middle of the town." Having been dependent on the car in the wilds of North Yorkshire to transport her work about, she is delighted at being able to walk everywhere in Cambridge. Her work reflects the inspiration of the West Riding of Yorkshire. She is currently making large detailed etchings of allegorical subjects, and is about to have an exhibition at Trumpington Gallery.

Eden Street the Latin Quarter of Cambridge? Perhaps. Mrs Sally Jones is a potter, and next door to Juliet de Gaye is the sculptor Keith Bailey. Then, of course, there is Constable's the stained glass works, further up towards Melbourne Place. Constable's was once a chapel for the Seventh Day Adventists. The baptism pit is under the floor in the workshop, covered up with glass. The firm still does a lot of local work. At the moment it is repairing some leaded lights in windows at Trinity College. There is glass by Constable's in Holy Trinity Church, in St Andrew's the Great, and in the south aisle of Milton Church – a small window depicting Jacob's Dream.

You can't go to Eden Street without looking in at the Elm Tree, where Françoise Mattock has built up a successful business in the last four years. The pub was rebuilt after a disastrous fire in 1976. "We call it the village here. Everybody knows everyone and they all help each other," she said. Fate has funny ways. Searches in local archives reveal that there was an earlier destructive fire at the Elm Tree, in November 1886. The *Cambridge Chronicle and University Journal* for 12 November records some details: "Mr Larkin, his wife and children effected an exit into the street, which was accomplished with some difficulty owing to the dense quantity of smoke which was rolling up the staircase. In Orchard Street they dressed as well as they were able. The Volunteer Fire Brigade dealt with the fire and a Mr Wright of Eden Street received the family into his house." Kindnesses still persist and are talked about, at the Elm Tree and at the Cricketers, and, of course, at Eden Street's local shop, John Cook's, which locals call the "Gossip Shop".

24 Fitzroy Street

3 September 1981

Fitzroy Street, in the heart of the Kite, was developed in the early years of the last century on what were, before the Enclosure Act of 1806–7, the Barnwell Fields of Cambridge. It is named after Augustus Henry Fitzroy, Duke of Grafton, who was Chancellor of the University. The duke died in 1811, but his name will live on in the Grafton Centre, the new name for the revitalised Kite, which it is hoped will emerge Phoenix-like from the rubble of demolition. The earlier name of the street, when there were only a few buildings in it, was Blücher

Fitzroy Street in the 1930s: these shops were opposite Laurie and McConnal's. "Hitler gets British reply", says the bill outside the newsagents

Row, a topical name then, because the expansion of the street took place at the close of the Napoleonic Wars. Wellington Street immortalises another hero. The Kite area, as we used to know it, has met its Waterloo. An atmosphere of battle hangs over the area as the east end of Fitzroy Street comes down and landmarks disappear.

The lower east end of Fitzroy Street, from its junction with James Street as far as East Road, was never so prosperous as the upper end. "Here were terraces of neat little houses and small shops, divided here and there by courts and passages containing two or three houses, and interspersed by public houses," writes Enid Porter in her article on Fitzroy Street and Burleigh Street. She points out

George Moon's shop, which thrived in the period between the wars. Men would buy a "halfpenny collar and halfpenny dickie" to go with their Sunday suits

that there were once nine public houses in the street – the Cherry Tree, the Danish Flag, the Fitzroy Arms, the Ancient Druids, the Duke of Wellington, the Harp, the Queen's Arms, the Golden Cross and, probably the earliest of them all, the Old English Gentleman. In the 1870s that east end of Fitzroy Street was the home of college servants, butchers, bakers, tailors, sawyers, shoemakers and a whitesmith. According to the street directory for 1874, a George Chapman had an "Umbrella Hospital" at 49 Fitzroy Street. Thomas Legge was a popular local baker at no. 12.

The local school was the British School at the corner of Christchurch Street, and on the other side of the road up towards East Road was a jam factory, originally that of Spencer, Ernest and Co., and later used by Chivers for roasting coffee and chicory. It was taken over during the first world war by the Army as a store. Latterly it was a brush factory, and finally, before demolition, a warehouse.

The Working Men's Club and Institute, at the corner of Fitzroy Street and East Road, was founded in 1862; its building was completed in 1873. Miss Porter says in her article that "The institute, through its library, the holding of lectures and classes, and the arrangement of exhibitions of local trades and crafts, played an important educational role in this largely working class area of Cambridge, as well as providing an alternative social centre to the public houses." (For more about the Club, see East Road.) One of the first two cinemas in Cambridge was above the Working Men's Club. In the 1930s opposite the club was a men's outfitters and dress-shop owned by a former mayor, E.O. Brown.

Mr Percy Moon, whose father George Moon ran Moon and Co., drapers, at what used to be 107 Fitzroy Street (the street was renumbered in 1920 and Moon's became no. 45), has clear memories of life in Fitzroy Street at the turn of the century. He remembers the two pawnbrokers near his father's shop. "There was Norman Bradley at 113 and Frederick Morley at 101 and 102. The women used to go into Morley's on a Saturday to get the suits out so that their husbands could go to church on a Sunday morning. On a Sunday morning the men would call at my father's shop, saying 'please, Mr Moon, can I have a halfpenny collar and a halfpenny dickie'" (shirt front). Percy Moon is 82 now. He lives with his wife at 23 March Lane, Cherry Hinton, but his roots are in the Kite. He and his wife were married at Christ Church. Mr Moon practised as a surgical technician up to the end of the last war. He has several stories to tell about Fitzroy Street.

Perhaps the most exciting is the legend, as he cautiously calls it, of the buried treasure. "Legend has it that there was a fortune buried in the cellar of our house in Fitzroy Street. The demolition boys had just about reached what used to be Moon's [in 1874 it was Daniel Buttress, the confectioners] when I was in the street last week. Perhaps they should remove the floorboards with care." Verlander's hardware shop at 23 Fitzroy Street (after 1920, nos. 70 and 72) was a local landmark on account of the famous tin kettle that hung above the door. Percy Moon remembers as a boy seeing the kettle being made at the back of the shop. He also remembers Mrs Mansfield who sold fireworks on Guy Fawkes

Day. "She would charge a penny for a Chinese Cracker." Beer was twopence a pint at the Ancient Druids and fish twopence and a portion of chips a penny at the Fitz Fried Fish Shop near the junction with Gold Street. Percy Moon bought dancing pumps at Tylers in Fitzroy Street for 1s 6d to wear when he went dancing at the Tipperary Club in Wellington Street.

Mr Moon speaks affectionately of W. Thompson and Sons, the furniture shop on the corner of Fitzroy Street and City Road, where the Salvation Army used to play. Thompsons are one of the oldest furnishers in Cambridge. "My great-great-grandfather who established the business was a cabinet maker in Willow Place," said Mr Peter Frederick Thompson, the present owner. "These premises were occupied in the early 1850s and bought by my grandfather in 1881. They were burnt down both in 1899 and 1902. The story goes that my grandfather was loaned money by Mr Bailey of Bailey and Tebbutt, the brewers, to rebuild the shop. It was then that living accommodation was built above." Peter Thompson took over the business when he came back from the war in September 1945. "My father died in March 1940 and Alderman P.J. Squires who had been with the firm since the age of 14 kept the doors open during the war. He was well over 70 when war broke out."

There is no doubt that Thompsons had a touch of the Harrods about them in the early days. A laudatory article in *The Gentleman's Journal and Gentlewoman's Court Review* for 29 May 1909, part of a local shopping guide featuring Cambridge, speaks of William Thompson and Son offering "value for money": "The handsome main premises of the Firm, with their 40 feet of frontage to Fitzroy Street and their 90 feet to City Road, embrace every department of the house furnishing industry, affording admirable opportunities for tastefully equipping the home . . . Especially attractive is the bed-room furniture, a glance at the suites in Chippendale, Sheraton, walnut, white enamel, and fumed oak being sufficient to show how far we have advanced from the sheer ugliness characteristic of the Early Victorian period. . . . A special branch is reserved for new and second-hand perambulators, mail carts and push carts. Where the convenience of customers requires it, any of the goods can be had on the hire-purchase system . . . Yet another branch of the enterprise is the supply of furniture and decorations for balls and other festivities. Amongst their other work in this direction the Firm provided the decorations for the Mayor's Reception at the Guildhall in 1908." Peter Thompson remembers the "big line" they used to do in furnishings for May Balls. "We

LEFT: *Looking up Fitzroy Street to the Grafton Centre, which was officially opened by Her Majesty the Queen on 16 May 1984 (ABOVE)*

provided Chinese lanterns, braziers and men on duty to keep the braziers going. I did ten May Balls in 1946." (A quick post-war revival in May Balls!)

Until 1931 Thompsons relied on horses for their transport, although they had bought their first motor vehicle in 1928. There was no parking problem in the Kite in those days. "Until well into the thirties my father used to park his car at the side door in City Road and there were no other cars in the street," said Peter Thompson, who recalls his penny ride on the Ortona green buses from the station to his home in Brunswick Gardens. He used to get to work in Fitzroy Street from his home by slipping through Fitzroy Lane at the side of Augustus Barnett, formerly the site of Norman Bradley's. "I can remember buying a second-hand pair of riding breeches for 5 shillings at Norman Bradley's," he said.

Another famous shop in Fitzroy Street to be destroyed by fire was Laurie and McConnal, which opened in 1883 in the former drapery, china and hardware premises of Samuel Young. Its premises were destroyed by a disastrous fire in 1903. But, as Miss Porter reminds us, rebuilding took place at once, and led to the erection of the attractive little bandstand still to be seen on the top of the store. Let's hope that is not going to come down. "From it the Cambridge Town Band used to play for the entertainment of Saturday shoppers, while teas were served on the roof garden. A sixpenny ham tea was a favourite speciality." Mrs Patricia Hawes, who works in Dixons, the popular Kite bakery, used to be an assistant at Laurie and McConnal. Christmas time and the decorations was the highspot for her, as it was for many Cambridge people.

Next door to Laurie and McConnal was the grocery and chemist's business of Joseph Sturton, the developer of Sturton Town. Further up from Sturton's just before Moon the drapers and Starr the photographers (Moon and Starr was a local joke) was Elijah Tarrant's, the sweet stores. Mrs Tarrant made delicious ice cream, which was very popular with the Fair people at Midsummer Fair time. Next door to Starr's, back in the days of the first world war, was the tobacconist Alfred Suttle, who was also in shipping and emigration and acted as the Great Northern and Great Eastern Railway receiving office. He had lunch with his son on board the Titanic just before it set sail from Liverpool on its fatal maiden voyage.

No. 104 (no. 53 following renumbering and recently demolished – perhaps we can expect a plaque in the Grafton Centre) was the first premises of W. Heffer and Sons, the famous bookshop with a multi-million pound turnover. William Heffer, the founder, opened there in 1872 as a stationer and newsagent, having started in business as a licensee of a public house in Burleigh Street, a job which was unpalatable to him but which enabled him to support his wife and family. It was the local vicar of the parish of St Andrew the Less who rescued him from the pub and helped him to get established in the shop, where he and his family lived and worked for 37 years. The stationery business continued in Fitzroy Street when the book business moved to Petty Cury. No. 103 Fitzroy Street was a sub-post office opened by William Heffer in 1886.

Anecdotes about Fitzroy Street mostly emphasise the neighbourliness of the area. Mr Barry Hobbs, whose daughter Josephine is an assistant in the invaluable local history library, the Cambridgeshire Collection, moved into Fitzroy Street in 1939. He remembers the evacuees from London, some of whom stayed on after the war. Mr Hobbs and his friends established the Cambridge Boys Club in Fitzroy Street in the early 1950s, thereby reinforcing a nice reputation as good helpful lads who always had time to run errands for elderly people. Among the local characters who stick in his mind are Bill Whitehead, the local greengrocer who was also the local unofficial bookie. He used to sit behind the receipt of customs, as it were, wearing a hard-topped bowler hat and accepting bets. Quite a far cry from the new Corals next to the Grafton Centre's information office further down on the corner of Eden Street!

It is hoped that the development of Fitzroy Street will take account of the traditions and reputations established in this once important street. Perhaps it will become important once again.

25 Burleigh Street

8–22 March 1984

Burleigh Street, where local traders have battled on in the face of the Kite redevelopment, putting up with adverse conditions during the construction of the Grafton Centre in adjacent streets, was originally laid out in the early years of the 19th century on part of the nursery called the Garden of Eden (see Eden Street).

It was named after the carrier James Burleigh, mayor of Cambridge in 1799, who lived in the large house in Newmarket Road later occupied by the Star Brewery. He gave his name to James Street too. A carrier and landowner with a patriotic character, James Burleigh offered 60 of his horses and eight wagons for the defence of the realm in case

The Forester's public house on the corner of Burleigh Street and City Road, a late Victorian view

Britain was invaded during the Napoleonic Wars. He was a Fellow of the Society of Antiquaries, and also a member of the Cambridge Volunteers.

Burleigh Street first became built up in the first half of the 19th century. In the Victorian era it was a street of artisans and small shopkeepers, in fact it has always been a trading street. A walk down Burleigh Street in 1874, eight years before the Cambridge Co-operative Society moved into the street, would have taken the visitor into the heart of a busy area serving the requirements of the local residents. There was an upholsterer and mattress maker, John Evans Jnr, at no. 1. His father John Evans Snr, who lived next door, was a cabinet maker. Then came William Carlish at no. 3, one of two butchers in the street. No. 4 on the east side of the street was the John Barleycorn public house, which was bought by

Burleigh Street before the Grafton Centre

the Co-op in 1882. Benjamin Rayment, the well-known straw hat and bonnet manufacturer and "leghorn presser" had his shop at no. 5. (The *OED* says leghorn was "a straw plaiting for hats and bonnets, made from a particular kind of wheat, cut green and bleached, and imported from Leghorn in Tuscany".) J. Freeman, the painter and glazier, occupied no. 6, Henry Whitehead, the bookbinder, no. 7 and E. Williamson, the tin and iron worker, no. 8.

Local residents would have gone to William Royston's general shop at no. 9 for their groceries. From no. 9 to no. 39 and the junction with Burleigh Place lived three college servants and two college cooks, four shoemakers, a glove cleaner, and two tailors, all of whom would have served the undergraduates at the University, as would the groom at no. 26, Alfred Baines. There was also a baker and a general dealer in that stretch of the street. Their customers would have included the plasterers, coal merchants, builders, paper hangers and engine drivers who lived in this working man's part of Cambridge.

There were five public houses in Burleigh Street in 1874. You could slake your thirst at the Burleigh Arms, the John Barleycorn, the John Bull at no. 50, the Oak at no. 71 or the Forester's at no. 74.

The appearance of Burleigh Street began to change with the growth of the Cambridge Co-operative Society, now having a face-lift on the west side of the street. Enid Porter tells the story in her article on Fitzroy Street and Burleigh Street: "It was in February, 1868, that the first meeting of the Cambridge Provident Industrial Society was held, largely through the enthusiasm of a group of the many shoemakers who earned a living in Cambridge at that time, making hand-sewn boots for undergraduates. The meeting was held at no. 2 City Road, the home of Charles Nightingale, bootmaker, and in the June of that year a president, committee, auditors and trustees were formally elected. By December, 33 people had taken £1 shares in the society. This number increased to 50 early in 1869, when co-operative trading began in a room rented at no. 8 City Road." In the first year sales totalled more than £1,000, and business grew so quickly that in 1871 no.

11 Fitzroy Street, next to the former Eden Baptist Chapel, was taken as a store and the society joined the Co-operative Wholesale Society.

In 1882 the society made its first move into Burleigh Street by buying the John Barleycorn. By 1898, it had acquired stores and an assembly room on the opposite side at nos. 62 to 68, where a row of small shops had been. Burleigh Street became the Co-op's headquarters in 1908, the range of departments there giving local people the chance to buy all they needed in one place. From the turn of the century, trading operations increased generally in Burleigh Street. There were more butchers – George Prior at no. 42a, George Clark at no. 73, and Edward Symonds at no. 18. Fishmongers and fruiterers, in particular Whitehead's, were among the popular local shops. Food, clothing, footwear and furniture were all available for the local residents, and at cheaper prices than in the town centre. Shops changed hands much less frequently in those days. Mr Tony Chapman of Greystoke Court, who was born at 1 Burleigh Street in 1919, writes that his father was in business there as a shoemaker and repairer for over 30 years, from about 1909 until his death in 1944. Mr Chapman can remember the sheep and pigs being delivered to the slaughterhouse in Burleigh Place every Monday.

There cannot be many Cambridge parents who haven't at one time or another been wheedled by their children into Townsend's toy and cycle shop in Burleigh Street to buy miniature Star Wars figures – a modern phenomenon – or that extravagant purchase – a new bicycle. Townsend's have been part of the Burleigh Street scene for more than 20 years. They moved into the Kite in 1963 from premises in Norfolk Street, where John Albert Townsend, whose father kept the Royal Engineer public house in Norfolk Street, started his cycle-making business in 1895. According to his grandson Roy, "My grandfather's enamelling shop in Norfolk Street was originally a cowshed with a pantile roof. The reason was that when he first married he started in the dairy business with his own herd of cows. His wife's family were country people, millers in fact." Grandfather Townsend tried his hand as a dairyman for two years before investing his energies and savings in the cycle business which has become a Cambridge institution. He started the firm with a colleague called Loker. They made their name as the manufacturers of the Light Blue Bicycle which, like a good suit, was made to measure. As Roy Townsend puts it, "The frames were built to fit you." John Albert devoted his working life to the manufacture of the Light Blue.

Roy Townsend has his grandfather's own personal bicycle on display in the shop. It has a big

Mr Arthur Hutchens, manager, with Linda Rosier (centre) and Andrea Jackson at Curtis the butchers

100-tooth chainwheel (it was made to celebrate the turn of the century) and its original colours were red, white and blue. Although John Albert allowed his son George to race the cycle occasionally, the founder used it himself every day right up until his death in 1942. The business was inherited by his son Christopher Almeric, father of Roy; he started it up again in 1945 after the second world war. In Norfolk Street Townsend's occupied a shop and a house – nos. 32 and 34. The premises were interconnected, which made working arrangements satisfactory. Christopher Almeric and his wife Miriam lived in one part, Roy and his wife Julie in the other. Today Roy, Julie, Miriam and grandson Lloyd are all partners in the business. Roy Townsend explains how they began to sell toys. "When K.G. Mason moved out of Norfolk Street into Burleigh Street at the time of the East Road–Staffordshire Street development, we acquired his two empty shops from the Council and spent £50 on filling the windows up with toys. My mother and her sister took over the running of the toys. Now it represents the major side of

A Co-op van in King's Parade in the 1920s

our business." Then the Townsends also became refugees from the building operations in and around Norfolk Street. They bought 15 Burleigh Street from the Browns, who had a dress shop there. The shop had belonged originally to G. Love and Son, the auctioneers, valuers and furniture removers, and there was a stable at the back where Mr Love used to keep his horse. Mrs Miriam Townsend remembers how Burleigh Street was in pre-Kite blight days. "When I first came up here there were five or six grocers I could go to and several butchers." There is still one family butcher's left in Burleigh Street – Curtis, the traditional pork butcher's, which opened there in 1945. The business occupies nos. 44 and 45, which were formerly divided into two, one half being used by J.H. Prior, the pork butcher, whose shop opened in 1909, and the other half having been over the years the Burleigh Arms public house, a second-hand furniture store and a tea bar.

Terence Wines have been in Burleigh Street for more than 20 years, too. Mr Terence Zarattini, who used to work at Matthews' grocer's shop in Trinity Street, started the business, the first in a small private group, in 1963. Now there are other branches, in Bedford, Oxford, Colchester and King's Lynn.

Mrs Lynn Hunt, Mr Zarattini's daughter, who has managed the shop for 13 years, regrets the passing of the old Fitzroy–Burleigh Street era. "It really did work when it was a hotch-potch of small local shops run by local traders. It had a certain charm, and was a good secondary shopping area with a lot of grocers, four butchers and somewhere where people came to shop for everyday things."

For generations of people the Co-op has been the "universal provider". In the days when everything was delivered by van that was a pretty fair claim! There can be few people who know more about the Cambridge Co-operative Society than Mr Donald Nelson who, after 51 years with the society, has become its unofficial archivist and social historian. A little upstairs study in his home in Beaumont Road is a miniature museum with copies of staff rule books and photographs of winning Co-op football teams among the items on display.

Donald Nelson started at the Co-op in Burleigh Street on 22 July 1927, the day after he left Milton Road School at the age of 14. His mother was a "great co-operator", and a "keen worker on the educational committee of the co-operative movement". He began as an errand boy in the grocery department. "But after the first morning I went on to the bakery as a van boy. There was no such thing as an apprenticeship." The bakery was over in James Street in those days. Since 1935 the James Street premises have been the headquarters of the Beehive Social Club. Mr Nelson became the club secretary in 1961.

After a spell as a van boy, Donald Nelson returned to the grocery department in Burleigh Street as an errand boy. "There were five or six errand boys at the Co-op in those days," he said. "It was one boy's job to feed the cats there. You had to collect the lites from the butcher, cook them and feed the cats. It was a matter of keeping the vermin down." Then for two years he was an errand boy in the Newnham Co-op in Grantchester Street. "I used to deliver with a hand cart from Newnham to the pre-

fabs which replaced the old First Eastern Hospital, now Burrell's Walk. The hours were strict: 8.30–1; 2.15–6 and 7 on Friday and Saturday. Thursday was a half day and the total number of hours worked was 44 a week. The extra quarter of an hour at lunchtime was for taking your overalls on and off. Sweeping up was part of the job, but it began after the shop closed."

In the early thirties Mr Nelson came back to Burleigh Street – "the hub of Co-op trading" – and worked as a junior in the despatch department at the rear of the grocery hall. "In those days we delivered all over the country, so there were quite a number of us in despatch. On Fridays and Saturdays we went into the store to work behind the counter." He continued in Burleigh Street until war broke out, when he went into the Royal Air Force. Between 1946 and 1955 he was manager of Co-op branches in Cherry Hinton Road and Milton Road, before returning as central grocery manager to Burleigh Street, when it was still the headquarters of the

The new-look, pedestrianised Burleigh Street created by the development of the Grafton Centre

Cambridge Co-op. In 1958 he was appointed as the first shops inspector for the Co-op in Cambridge, and in 1960 he became the assistant grocery manager in the warehouse in Sleaford Street. During his last five years at the Co-op, before his retirement in July 1979, he was in charge of the food office which dealt with invoices.

Archives and account books show just how crucial the society was to many families. "In 1927 when I started," said Mr Nelson, the "dividend was 1*s* 8*d* in the pound. People were able to save, and clothe their families, with that money." He looks back on his time with the Co-op with a real sense of pride. He had a lot of fun too, particularly in the thirties. "We had so many social events in those days – whist drives and dances in the Co-op Hall above the shop in Burleigh Street" (now the staff dining hall). Mr Nelson remembers another occasion – when he organised a complete train to take the staff and their families to Southsea. "Four hundred and fifty people joined the train. In the front of the train, two carriages had had their seats taken out for a rock'n'roll session." There were many outings like that and social life for Co-op employees has always been active.

Mrs Marlene Lask, whose parents Julius and Paulina Goldwater opened a menswear shop called Pauline's opposite the Co-op in 1930, recalls that "The Co-op in those days had iron shutters on the doors and an enormous food hall in the centre with marble floors and separate counters for different provisions." Mrs Lask was born in Fitzroy Street opposite the Eden Baptist Chapel. Her parents, known locally as "Mr and Mrs Pauline", had opened Pauline's Dress Shop in Fitzroy Street in 1929. The shop used to be Moon's. "My parents were in business in Burleigh Street for 39 years and in Fitzroy Street for 40 years." During the war, the streets were full of soldiers and airmen – her father supplied them with many of their clothing requirements such as lanyards and badges – and there was a lot of hustle and bustle. Of course, at night "everything went pitch black". The gas lamps were extinguished and if you went out you had to take a torch. There were two air raid shelters in Burleigh Street. Residents celebrated VE Day with a "super party" in Adam and Eve Street. Mrs Lask remembers going to it in fancy dress.

The Forester's public house was the popular haunt of the Fair people when they came to Midsummer Common. "They packed into the pub and spilled out in to the street, there were so many of them." What a lively trading street it was in those days. Then followed years of uncertainty and decay. Now, however, Burleigh Street is being rejuvenated, a vital part of the area around the Grafton Centre.

Bibliography of published sources cited in this volume

(Vol. I contains a more extensive bibliography)

Amey, Leonard, 'Barnwell Fields: Medieval Ownership and Post-Enclosure Development', *Cambridgeshire Local History Society Bulletin* XXXVIII (1983), 13–25

Barnard, A., 'A Description of the Star Brewery, Cambridge', in *The Noted Brewers of Great Britain and Ireland*, IV (London, 1891), 462–81

The Cambridgeshire Technical College and School of Art 1858–1958 (Cambridge, n.d.)

Chaffin, D.E., 'Charles Humfrey and Early Nineteenth Century Building in Cambridge', thesis, University of Cambridge Faculty of Architecture (1963)

Chater, Josiah, *Victorian Cambridge: Josiah Chater's Diaries*, ed. Enid Porter (London, 1975)

Danckwerts, Peter V., 'The Inheritors of Barnwell Priory', *Proceedings of the Cambridge Antiquarian Society* LXX (1981 for 1980), 211–27

Gray, Arthur B., *Cambridge Revisited* (Cambridge, 1921)

Hall, Catherine, 'Maids' Causeway', *Cambridge Civic Society Newsletter* XIII.8 (1982), 11–13

Humfrey, Charles, *Particulars and Conditions of Sale of . . . Mansion House*, 6 August 1846

Jebb, Eglantyne, *Cambridge: A Brief Study in Social Questions* (Cambridge, 1906)

Jones, Charles Alfred, *A History of the Jesus Lane Sunday School, Cambridge (1827–1877)* [Cambridge, 1877]

Keynes, Florence Ada, *By-Ways of Cambridge History*, 2nd edn (Cambridge, 1956)

Mitchell, E., *Notes on the History of Parker's Piece, Cambridge* [Cambridge, 1984]

O'Neill, P.M., 'St Columba's York Street Mission', *Cambridgeshire Local History Council Bulletin* XXXVI (1981), 25–35

Porter, Enid, 'Fitzroy Street and Burleigh Street, Cambridge', *Cambridgeshire Huntingdon and Peterborough Life*, July 1971, 22–3

Royal Commission on Historical Monuments, *An Inventory of the Historical Monuments in the City of Cambridge* (London, 1959)

Stokes, H.P., *Outside the Barnwell Gate* (Cambridge, 1915)

[Sturton Street] *Primitive Methodist Chapel, Sturton Street, Cambridge, Jubilee Celebrations 1875–1925 Souvenir Handbook* [Cambridge, 1925]

Trewin, J.C., *Robert Donat: A Biography* (London, 1968)

Unwin, F.T., *Pimbo and Jenny in Old Cambridge* (Cambridge, 1978)

Widnall, Samuel Page, *A Gossiping Stroll through the Streets of Cambridge* (Grantchester, 1892)